D1179821

THE PERSONALITY OF THE YOUNG CHILD

THE PERSONALITY OF THE

young child

AN INTRODUCTION FOR PUZZLED PARENTS

by MARGARET A. RIBBLE, M. D.

COLUMBIA UNIVERSITY PRESS

New York and London

COPYRGHT © 1955 COLUMBIA UNIVERSITY PRESS

First printing 1955
Third printing 1962

LIBRARY OF CONGRESS CATALOG CARD NUMBER: 55-10540

MANUFACTURED IN THE UNITED STATES OF AMERICA

contents

17308

vi

CONTENTS

THE PERSONALITY OF THE YOUNG CHILD

introduction

Thoughtful parents today, as well as educators and psychologists, continue to press these urgent questions: What can we do to insure the healthy growth of the child's mind and personality? Can painful and crippling emotional difficulties be avoided? Why does a youngster become delinquent?

Thanks to the diligent and untiring research of Freud and his followers we are today much better informed about the forces at work in psychological development in early childhood. We have been brought face to face with the fact that the biological urges of sex and aggression are present in the child from birth. Perhaps of even greater importance is the recognition that in the budding ego of the small human being lies the potentiality to sublimate much of the energy from these basic urges into rewarding emotional and social outlets and into self-completion through learning.

Parents who have the will and the courage to acquire the necessary background of knowledge concerning the early development of personality will be able to prevent the appearance of many personality problems. Recognition, first, of the changing modes of expression of instinctual energy in the small child as he matures, together with skill in diverting this valuable energy into functional use through the medium of a warm relationship, is the essence of early psychological parenthood.

Firsthand daily observation provides a special opportunity to guide a child at critical stages of development. If parents join forces with psychiatrists and educators for mutual interchange, new knowledge will undoubtedly be gained by all, so that problems of personality development may be clarified.

In an earlier book, *The Rights of Infants*, the writer discussed some of the psychological needs of babies. The present volume carries that theme forward to the toddler and the pre-school child. Its aim is to point out to parents their essential role of understanding and guidance as the toddler encounters new forms of experience and comes into possession of new faculties and feelings.

There are few specific rules for the psychological care of young children, but new information is available and fresh wisdom is to be gained in its application to the individual child.

For successful guidance of children in the age group here discussed, parents must know that certain experiences in early life may intensify instinctual urges to pathological proportions. Conversely, lack of opportunity to exercise natural functions freely (such as sucking, biting, climbing) as they emerge may seriously impede the orderly course of development of self.

In the areas of sex and aggression, intelligent guidance is imperative at the outset if later difficulty is to be avoided.

Permissiveness without direction is as harmful as neglect. It leads to license, not freedom, and is as disturbing to a healthy child as is the old method of severe restriction.

one

GETTING PERSPECTIVE

In our twentieth-century culture the first years of a
child's life are rarely thought of as a period of vital
significance for his mental development. The decisive
role of parents in promoting the first stages of psychological growth is seldom recognized. Young parents themselves do not usually consider this phase of
their lives as one of special psychological creativeness,
during which they observe and take a dynamic part in

the personality development of their children. On the contrary there is an unfortunate and widely held concept of these years as being predominantly a time of sacrifice and deprivation, a time to be lived through gracefully or met with fortitude and gotten over. Emphasis has been placed on the giving-up of leisure time or of accustomed social pleasures, on frequent and unpredictable interruptions of sleep, on at least a two-year period of washing small garments and sterilizing bottles. Often a truly biblical sense of self-punishment can be detected in the attitude of young parents.

There is, of course, some truth in these present-day illusions, for without serious thought and constructive planning in advance any creative undertaking can deteriorate into mechanical and wasteful routine. Without some basic knowledge of the subject, particularly one as important as the fostering of a child's mental growth, there is little chance of satisfaction in the undertaking, however intuitive the parents may be. Even the most gifted painter must learn his technique, the most talented musician must study and practice endless hours and continue to do so throughout his entire career.

The psychological care of a child in the early stages of maturing is indeed a creative project for the parent. It requires skill, keen observation, deep and controlled personal feeling, and a readiness to observe with warmth and sympathy the needs of the individual child. Much time must be devoted to the undertaking, sometimes around the clock. Nevertheless, well-planned arrangements for leisure are important for both mother and father—for this must be a joint project if it is to be a success. The giving of time and self to the child while he is attaining the first levels of independence is an obvious part of early parenthood, but to make this gift effective neither parent need become too sacrificial. The father or mother who is persistently drained of well-being and energy can be disturbing to the child. Parenthood is not an atonement but rather an enrichment which comes with true emotional creativeness.

A young infant is not ready to fit into the convenience of routine family life; he is psychologically unorganized. His maturing may be delayed or endangered by the family activities; and the family comfort may be greatly disturbed by the presence of the wailing child whose needs are a mystery. However, if the pertinent facts of early psychological growth are well known and understood, and if parents have within themselves a reasonable amount of emotional stability, the venture of psychological parenthood can yield deep satisfaction. Introducing the toddler to the world of people and things about him in a spirit matching his own takes true dramatic inventiveness.

On the other hand, if young parents experience a gloomy sense of deprivation rather than an optimistic attitude of finding new ways of relating themselves to life and new adventure in the process of living, the feeling life of the child may be adversely affected.

It has been generally agreed by those who have studied child development carefully that the most important stimulus to the growth and maturing of a healthy personality in the child is sound relationship with both parents. His basic capacity for response and for forming and maintaining good emotional and social relationships throughout life is rooted and patterned in these early beginnings. Hence, the creative function of parents is not finished when the child is born. From the psychological point of view it has just begun. In much the same way that the body of the foetus develops inside the mother, absorbing what is needed for organic maturing, so the mental life of the child is energized by means of the close relationship with his parents. For this reason it is particularly important to consider the subject of "psychological parenthood," not with the idea of pointing an accusing finger at mothers and fathers because of the mistakes they may make, but rather to emphasize their personal importance for the child's well-being and basic happiness and for his effectiveness as a future member of the human family. Consistent warmth, wisdom, and understanding on the part of the parents must be the basis of this relationship, for it is the means by which the young human being can be led later on to accept the various requirements of the culture in which he is to live without too much conflict and strain.

We think of parenthood biologically as a stage of adult development which comes about with the maturing and stabilizing of the sex life. Psychologically we know that the personal and emotional adjustments necessary for successful marriage are an important part of preparation for being a parent. Thoughtful young people today are well aware of their own need for more and better preparation if they are to guide their children in attaining emotional maturity and in avoiding unnecessary frustrations which cause unhappiness and inefficiency. They would like to be assured that their child will have a satisfactory maturing of the mental faculties with which he is endowed, and especially they hope to help him avoid the emotional disturbances which so often disrupt the intellectual life of the child and impair the urge to learn. The second part of the preparation for parenthood, then, is gaining sound knowledge of the early stages of the child's mental development.

The keynote to the understanding of early childhood is acceptance of the long period of mental immaturity. The brain at birth is the least developed (and the least ready to function) of the child's essential organs. Its structural units are all present and will mature in an orderly sequence: that is, new cells cannot be added after birth, but the maturing of the organic units and their linking together for functional use can be definitely promoted through understanding care and through protection against harmful experiences.

When the toddler begins to talk, his nervous system is still incomplete and exhibits a form of behavior that implies great instability. His mental life is closely geared to impressions of bodily comfort and pleasure and to the avoidance of pain. His wishes are coupled with deep bodily needs for nourishment and affectionate contact.

To be successful as parents, his father and mother need the capacity to love him because of his innate potentialities rather than to feel affection in spite of his lack of finish. Their love must be expressed in ways to which he can respond. In order to maintain the qualities of respect and consideration for the child's incompleteness his parents have the right to know what is going on in the maturing process. Morale is built up and ease of mind attained when parents "know the reason why."

The state of dependency which is the very essence of early childhood serves an important creative purpose both physiologically and psychologically. It gives the brain time to mature and catch up on its organic completion and also permits the early mental faculties of awareness and sensitivity to develop by means of the close relationship of the child with his parents. For this reason any attempts to make the child independent in the first two years of life before he can walk and talk can be definitely injurious. Progress in this direction can come only when there is good organic integration and growth of the nervous system.

Many parents, particularly mothers, enjoy deeply the early period of a child's complete dependency. However, it is wise to make sure that the adults do not prolong the period and thereby render more difficult the child's next step toward maturity. It is possible to "spoil" small children by continuing in excess the early mothering activities past the time when the child is ready to take an active part in furthering his own way of functioning. For example, the cradle is useful and comfortable in the first months of life but is less advantageous when the child is able to move his own body about. At six months a blanket on the floor for rolling and kicking is a great stimulus to muscular development. The playpen is a distinct aid in the period before creeping is far advanced. At this time the playpen is not a restriction to the child, but a promotion; its limited area in which he can climb to his feet, roll his body around safely, and manipulate the first toys is an important protection. The little creeper does not gain freedom by proceeding into places where there are untouchables, such as fireplaces, gas stoves, and electric sockets, and his sudden removal from such interesting objects is far more injurious than the restriction to a small area of experimentation.

The transition from the playpen to full room area of the nursery must be gradual, with the mother present to observe the nature of the child's interests and to protect him from bodily harm. To a small child freedom is not based on unlimited areas to explore but on a solid nervous integration and the gaining of good muscular coordination.

These excellent devices for the early care of the child—the cradle, the playpen, and the nursery—have unfortunately become associated with the ideas of restriction and of discipline against which there is at the present time vigorous reaction. Here it is necessary to consider the period of the child's development in which these items are appropriate.

The emergence from infantile passivity and helplessness when things were done to him and for him is a gradual process. His activities must be limited to an appropriate area where he is entirely safe. In the nursery, where the furniture and toys are entirely his, the toddler gets an important first sense of possession and property and is safely free to get acquainted with his small section of reality. This sort of freedom is not his in the family living room, where objects which he has discovered are repeatedly taken away from him and where the tension of adults who are rescuing valuables is highly disturbing to him.

The use of the cup and spoon and even self-feeding are often achieved at the age of eight months. This marks good progress in development but should not be pushed too fast. Even at one year when the baby sits happily in his high chair at the family table, he tends to become overexcited so that the situation is entirely a social one and his own eating and that of the family are disturbed.

Eating his meals alone with his mother gives the child greater freedom and better appetite; food can be thoroughly explored and distinguished from other materials. It is good not to forbid the child to put his hands in food and smear it about. Since the mouth is the center of his functioning from the time of birth, it is an extremely important avenue for learning and discovering. Good manners and social behavior in connection with eating will come much later in the course of development.

Playing alone for short periods is important. At from one to two years of age, on awakening in the morning and after a nap, it is valuable to play alone in the crib or playpen for not more than half an hour. When the child is refreshed by sleep is the ideal time for him to initiate play of his own with a few simple toys which have been placed within reach on the bedside table. However, leaving him to play alone later in the day because mother has company or is busy can give a young child the feeling of being excluded or not wanted. The child from ten to twenty months who wakes up alone in his own room and plays with his toys is better adjusted than the one who is immediately picked up and brought into bed to frolic with parents. Before he is two years old, long periods of being alone or with a new nurse are painful. He still needs parent or nurse to initiate activity or to function for him, because his chief energies are being utilized for inner growth, and therefore the protecting presence of a loving adult is vital.

Each child is a different individual. Thus one may be precocious muscularly, stand and even walk at ten months, but be slow in social response. Another may vocalize and speak a few words at a year but be slow in manipulating his body and getting on his feet. This may disturb parents so that they attempt too vigorously to even up the imbalance.

Early psychological development is not a precise process in which one stage is lived through and left behind. Much of the baby trails along in the toddler, who frequently needs the privilege of "being a baby." Conversely, it can be seen that at any stage the next phase of maturing is beginning to show itself. Actually, parents must look in two directions at once, backward and forward. At the same time they must be keenly aware of current needs. This is one of the requirements which makes psychological parenthood complicated but interesting. A special skill is needed to keep proper perspective on traits which are about to emerge and at the same time to look back into the phase of development immediately preceding and make allowances for incompleteness and for influences out of the past.

A four-year-old girl, faced all day with the stress of adjusting to visiting relatives, climbed into her mother's lap in the evening and said, "Mommie, rock me. I ain't big." Similarly, a sturdy toddler protested vigorously when his father carried him across a busy street; but a few minutes later, when the father stopped to speak with a friend whom the child did not know, the small boy insisted on being carried. He had become uneasy, and felt separated, out of touch, and suddenly alone, and therefore he needed a renewal of infant closeness in order to regain his equilibrium. Six months later he will use other tactics to divert attention to himself, by suggesting some action as by insisting, "Daddy, let's go!"

On a visit to unfamiliar relatives to whom his parents have proudly boasted of his advanced development a child may upset his glass of milk or refuse to eat something prepared especially for him. Later on he will demonstrate that he is far from "house broken." In the presence of too many unfamiliar circumstances controls are loosened, and the mature ways of conducting himself which so delighted his parents at home suddenly disappear. Yet parents know that in the familiar setting of home social ways are developing spontaneously in the child, and infantile helplessness is rarely resorted to.

An important concept to recognize and become familiar with in the earlier phases of maturing is that of *reversibility*. The maturing process is most vulnerable in the early years. When repeated or prolonged experiences of pain, hunger, or aloneness occur too often in the life of the young child his psychological growth is disturbed, he becomes disorganized, and automatically a tendency develops to revert to earlier ways of functioning which brought sure satisfaction. Thus, very often, he will resort to finger sucking. Reversibility lessens as personality becomes well coordinated, as when, for example, the child knows the reason for pain and understands that separation from a loved person is temporary. If many disturbances have occurred in the earlier periods of development the tendency to turn backward becomes exaggerated and continues through the period of adolescence and even into adult life.

Evidences of this regressive tendency do not appear at once in the child; the slipping back is insidious and may come to light in disordered forms of behavior or "habits" which are recognized only later. A particularly dramatic illustration of this automatic throwback in psychic development is to be seen when a new sibling is born and the older child has not been well prepared in advance. At the age of two this event is a shock which may go unrecognized by the parents at the time, but its results are clearly seen later in eating difficulties, hyperactivity, and often in exaggerated destructiveness.

There has been considerable discussion among psychologists as to the reasons for this strong tendency toward regression in the early life of the human child. "Birth trauma" is one of the factors that has received earnest attention. This "trauma" has had many interpretations. I am inclined to think that the most logical explanation is relative to the drastic change of bodily functions which takes place immediately after birth if the child is to survive. The prenatal child gets both oxygen and nourishment by way of the placenta, an organ which is discarded at birth. Before birth the physiological needs of the child are provided for him. After birth he must do his own breathing, and for this he needs the stimulus of his mother's care. Food and air must be taken in through the mouth, and the circulation rerouted and distributed to lungs and stomach, and also to the brain, which has to deal with incoming sensations from without and further stages of completion within.

This change in functional activities occurs also in the simpler mammals; these are not known to suffer from birth trauma, but they do not have before them the elaborate developmental task of bringing the higher brain into action and maintaining it, and they are endowed with stronger instincts for the maintenance of life. The energies of the baby must be immediately deflected toward the new physiological demands—above all, to the completion of brain building. This drastic change of bodily functions may not proceed smoothly and may cause considerable tension (manifested in constant crying that is difficult to soothe). The tendency to slip back into the simpler functioning of prenatal life remains strong. This view of birth trauma is quite different from the concept of mechanical injury to the nervous system.

A fundamental new concept has recently come into our thinking about the growth of mind and personality: the concept of life energy and the ways in which it expresses itself in human activities both physical and mental. This dynamic concept is helpful in keeping perspective on the behavior of the child as he develops through the early phases of psychological maturing.

Ours is an age of the study of energy in its varying forms. The energy of sound and its reception in radios and telephones have brought new interest and pleasure into our lives, even though many of us do not have complete knowledge of the nature of sound waves and how they are transmitted. In somewhat the same way we look at a television program for enjoyment and new information, leaving to the experts the knowledge of the way in which visual images, light and color, have been brought to us at the turn of the knob. Atomic energy holds the promise of unthought-of power provided we do not allow ourselves to be destroyed by it before its constructive uses are established.

In the field of life energy in human beings it is parents who need to become experts and to make sure that they understand as completely as possible the known forms of potential energy which take part in mental functioning and in the development of human personality. Three main types of life energy call for study and understanding by all whose aim is to guide the young child from the start into full use of his bodily and mental capacities. The first two are instinctual energies. Sexual energy, which throughout nature has its roots in the reproductive function, has a modified course of development in the human child until adolescence. During early life this basic creative urge contributes to the mental function of sensitivity and to the growth of awareness. It stirs and enriches the emotional capacity to love fully. Parents have the task, none too easy, of helping the child to deflect impulsive erotic urges when they tend to become exaggerated and to substitute play activities with family and playmates which yield other sorts of emotional and social satisfaction. This must be done without instilling feelings of guilt by moralistic disapproval. The task requires deep knowledge, understanding, and controlled affection on the part of parents.

The second type, aggressive energy, is nature's drive for defense and mastery and is expressed primarily through muscular activities. The tireless energies of the toddler need to be provided for and directed into vigorous body-building games to prevent their spilling over into destructiveness. Acquiring balance and skill in locomotion is the child's first mastery of his own body. He acts first and thinks later, yet in freedom of action important experience is gained, provided he is protected from hurt. Parents need to know that aggressive energy in the child contributes zest to constructive effort when it is directed from the beginning into positive forms of expression. A happy mastery of the body can lead naturally into mental effort and mastery, whereas forcible restriction of early bodily activity tends to increase the destructive tendencies in aggression because it interferes with a primal sense of personal freedom.

Last and perhaps most interesting because it is

most characteristically human is ego energy, the motive force of thinking and intelligence—of the self. Self-feeling begins to show itself in the child as higher areas of the brain mature and become linked up, re-energizing the various bodily capacities for feeling and action. Consciousness spreads as perceptions deepen, attention pushes forward, memory becomes evident, and all are synchronized into thinking. As this development proceeds the child sleeps somewhat less, becomes more alert, and is ready to participate in new experiences. This is the period of beginning psychological acquisitiveness, of the wish to know and link up something new with what is familiar in himself. It is characteristic of ego energy that it is not so insistent and vigorous as the instinctual urges to get pleasure and to go into action. Hence it is important that parents lead the toddler into simple new experiences which will widen his interests and enable him to get keen satisfactions through learning.

Three areas of personality are of especial concern to the toddler's parents: the instincts, the ego, and emotional relatedness. If all three are kept in mind and parents recognize how life energies are expressed during successive stages of mental growth, a much better perspective can be maintained on the course of the child's psychological maturing.

two

EARLY SEXUAL DEVELOPMENT

An age-old tabu surrounds the subject of childhood sexuality. For this reason it is extremely difficult for the average parent to break away from conventional prejudice and to accept the fact that all healthy children are from birth endowed with erotic impulses which are normal and valuable for psychologic maturing. The sex instinct is a biological inheritance upon which reproduction depends. But more than this it makes a large contribution during early life to the functional development of the body and mind.

Pleasure feeling is nature's "all's well" signal, her criterion of rightness that precedes the ability to appraise values and meanings. Vital and important functions carry a charge of pleasure energy which tends to insure their repeated performance. When parents set themselves against this natural force they are opposing a part of the life instinct. In order to guide a growing child it is necessary to recognize the expression of these primary feelings of the body without embarrassment or disapproval. This is where "sex education" begins.

The native sensuousness of a child is not centered at first in the genital organs but is diffused through the entire body. The strongest pleasure feelings are in the mouth, a fact which helps to insure the nutritional function and later on contributes to the development of speech. The eyes early become related to oral activity and their first focus is on the face of the mother, which comes to mean satisfaction of all needs —provided of course that she understands these needs. The ears soon come to share in this first combined relational and eating experience, and the hands gradually begin to grope. In this way a small baby first relates itself to the mother. The first diffuse sensuousness spreads and intensifies the specific sensations of sight, hearing, and touch. This is also the groundwork of the faculty of attention.

Sexuality is a progressive development. Under favorable circumstances it shifts in an orderly way from one area of the body to another as important functions become established. The mouth continues to be the chief pleasure and testing center for the child until speech is well established.

After the infant can sit up, the lower part of the body becomes more strongly activated with pleasure feeling; the feet are grasped, studied, and put into the mouth; the hands wander over the thighs and abdomen while the infant is being bathed and dressed, in a gesture which indicates early self-discovery. Toward the second year some of the first sensuousness of the mouth shifts to the functions of elimination, and the child shows increased awareness of bowel and bladder function. It is an interesting fact that readiness to begin the control of elimination usually coincides with the ability to stand alone and take the first steps.

Around the age of three the child's erotic feeling becomes centered more definitely in the sex organs, and periods of definite sex play can be observed. This is always accompanied in the mental sphere by fantasy, the first pleasure thinking. A child who has not sensed disapproval and who has not been laughed at will later on formulate these vivid sex fantasies verbally. These fantasies are based on early love feelings for the parents; often they are a continuation of the early babyhood contacts and caresses. In this way the child's mind spins a web of pleasure which cannot be taken from him even by disapproving adults.

The sex play and accompanying fantasy life of the third and fourth year are intermingled with the growing love feelings for parents and family. These feelings lead the child into what is known as the Oedipus complex, in which there is a miniature falling in love with the parent of the opposite sex and strong antagonism for the parent of the same sex. At this time the child has the difficult task of establishing a love relationship to parents and family from which sex is excluded.

We are aware that the young of our household pets and domestic animals mature differently and also rapidly without a quiescent period. The close physical relationship of the small domestic animal to its mother soon becomes overtly sexual and complete sexual maturity is reached at an early age, without a period of latency. In the young child the natural repression which takes place is due in part to a shifting of energy which makes possible the development of an all-important faculty which we call the capacity for sub-limation. This means that with the understanding help of parents the erotic impulses of the child can be at least partly diverted into family love and social interests.

These early phases of erotic development make a significant contribution at adolescence toward the establishment of a healthy adult sex life. The wish to develop and grow to be like the parents and to accept their cultural attitudes (in which sexuality is partially sublimated to intellectual and social creativeness) is the outcome of a good relationship in early childhood and of sound emotional ties within the family. Unfortunately it is rare that these phases of instinctual development reach an orderly maturing. More than any other physiological or psychological activity, sexuality is subject to distortion, exaggeration, or false suppression. As long as the tenet prevails that sex in early life is unnatural and evil and should therefore be eradicated, healthy development will continue to give way to emotional crippling. The capacity of the child to love fully with his emotions rather than with his body will thus be injured, and the important ego capacity to find a wider pleasure in learning will be damaged.

Because parents generally do not recognize the early stages of sex development, they will ask at this point why it is so important to know these facts. Will not nature and the growth process take care of these first stages of maturing? In any case, what can be done at such an early age to help the child understand himself and to avoid emotional damage?

To answer these questions we must return to the first stages of pleasure activity in the mouth. It is easy to see that here the need to suck is far beyond that of nutritional requirement. When this activity is not provided for and self-regulated, the sucking, which is a strong pleasure activity, often continues with vigor into the second year. Keeping sensuous urges geared to utility functions is an ideal aim. Some children have stronger oral urges than others. If the sucking urge is satisfied freely at the appropriate time, it diminishes naturally and tends to be partly replaced by chewing, grasping, looking, and other urges. Parents can provide experiences which further this displacement of functional energy. On the other hand, children whose oral urges have not been satisfied by free sucking and who somewhat later undergo frustrating experiences— separation in the second and third year from the mother, deprivation of a loved nurse, or the pain of an organic illness—will console themselves with sucking, regardless of whether or not they have been "thumb suckers" in early life. The pleasure-getting or tension-relieving function of the mouth may be retained, thus disturbing the orderly sequence of maturing.

Toward the end of the first year the small child begins to demonstrate his strong pleasure feeling in various parts of his own body. When he is naked or is being bathed, his fingers will wander over the navel and nipples, and also into the genital region. This is evident too while he is being diapered or put on the toilet. Usually the baby will look "questioningly" at his mother as he explores his body. Most parents unknowingly have a forbidding attitude toward these early touch activities. Often the wandering hand is removed vigorously, sometimes even with a slap and "No! No!" with the result that the child tends early to pursue these pleasure activities in secret. His relationship to his mother is disturbed. On the other hand, when the parent shows neither embarrassment nor disapproval, but rather smiles casually while gently diverting the child's attention and providing the small hand with a loved toy, the sensuous impulses will not gain exaggerated momentum nor will they drift into secret channels. This leaves the way open to the child for further expression of his bodily feelings and enables the parent to guide him more easily.

The attitude of our culture is still to reject childhood sexuality without further investigation. More recently a scant number of parents, in reaction, have adopted the attitude of permitting the child free sex play without attempting to direct him toward other sources of pleasure; this has met with equally damaging results. The middle path of deeper understanding and sympathetic diverting is as yet rarely attempted or achieved.

Many parents have such a deep dread of "sex habits" that they begin to disapprove of the child's most natural expression of bodily pleasure even at this early age. This unfortunate attitude leads the child to a misunderstanding of himself and later on to feelings of guilt and shame about natural functions. Further, it starts a rift in the relation with the parent and arouses a feeling of not being loved, which may have far-reaching effects.

Before the small child can formulate his feelings in words, his actions express certain needs. For example, a child of fourteen months began to resist violently being dressed and undressed. The same child showed great interest in dolls, but immediately took their clothes off and would play happily only with naked dolls. It turned out that this youngster had never been allowed to roll about without clothing before the bath, or to creep around naked in the room. The parents were overly shy and modest and felt that they could avoid the child's interest in his body functions, and particularly in his sex organs, by keeping him always dressed in the most secure of clothing, day and night. The bed covering was tightly pinned up and tucked in, so that the little hands would have no opportunity to explore the body or come in contact with the diaper and its contents. The child's aversion to dressing and undressing was overcome by arranging for him a play period without clothing before the bath each day and in play trunks at appropriate times, until he was able to formulate natural questions about the body. This early stamp of approval by the parent on the child's nakedness or freedom of bodily activity gives him the feeling—shared by his parents—that the body is good.

The functions of elimination give the child a strong erotic pleasure during the second year. This is the suitable time to begin toilet-training casually and gently. The toddler likes to be taken to the toilet and to be wiped or washed. If a potty-chair is conveniently placed, he will soon seat himself on it at intervals, provided he has been introduced pleasantly and without stress to the new procedure. Many children show exaggerated interest in the products of the body. A few, if left alone on the potty-chair, have a strong tendency, quite natural at this time, to play with the stools. This is by no means evidence of abnormality; but it is wise to avoid occasions for this and to divert the child into the more socially acceptable play with a sandbox, finger-paints, or modeling clay.

When the child begins to eat semisolid food, such as cereals, it is important to let him smear some of the food, put his hands into it, and get the feel of pliable material, for this is a natural interest at his age. In an earlier day, mothers who made bread encouraged this interest by giving the child a piece of dough to play with; the soft-rubber toys of today are a useful substitute. The parent who is fastidious and turns the child too quickly away from his interest in "what the body makes" and how he can urinate is apt to overemphasize these interests. Parents who are objective and not particularly concerned with exaggerated cleanliness in the first years are in a better position to bring the child through the processes of training to cleanliness in a leisurely way and without distortion of interest.

Children who have been subject to digestive upsets and have either constipation or diarrhea frequently or over a long period early show greatly increased erotic interest in elimination. When enemas or suppositories have been used frequently in the first or second year, toilet interest reaches a high pitch. The relationship to parent or nurse becomes involved with schemes to get this attention. The child often retains stools over long periods in order to get pleasurable attention, then loses control. A delay in the development of sustained control may result. Parents who understand the reason for this are less upset by a prolonged period of messiness and disorder in the child's activities and usually allow him to work through the period of delayed development by means of play activity. Such play may appear as interest in the excrement of animals, in endless taking of dolls and toy animals to the toilet, or as a prolonged interest in making mud pies, painting, and smearing.

A period of early exhibitionism with a strong urge to look at and show the body is a natural part of the self-discovery of the second year. It becomes more exciting when shared by a brother or sister. The early intimacies of bathing and dressing together may be quite harmless; if, however, these intimacies are continued without the presence of an adult, too much excitement is aroused, and the practice becomes anything but a matter-of-fact and casual sort of play.

Another question asked by parents at this stage is the following: "If frank expression of bodily pleasure feeling is natural and beneficial for a child, what harm can come when this early form of sex play is indulged in by siblings or playmates?" One answer is that pleasure and bodily excitement are increased by the eager participation of the playmate. Simple investigation and comparison progress to touching, and an all-absorbing demand for this sort of play is engendered. Latent sexuality is aroused which may disturb the child's progressive development. Frequent bodily contact between small children often results in seductions passed on from one child to another.

Between the ages of three and five, the child's erotic feelings become more definitely centered in the sex organs, and sex play is frequently seen if it has not been too rigidly discouraged. The child observes the parents closely and asks many questions as to why they sleep together and how they make babies. Usually at this time the child develops a strong love, accompanied by an urge for caressing and bodily contact with the parent of the opposite sex and an intense rivalry with the parent of the same sex.

This can be a very difficult period in the life of the child, unless he has been fortunate in having parents who have encouraged him to express to them his feelings and fantasies without shame or fear. The sex play that is a natural part of this period is not harmful; it rarely becomes exaggerated unless some earlier seduction experiences have occurred. On the other hand when parents have shown uneasiness and disapproval of early interest in the body, an acute sensitiveness develops in the child. He feels himself guilty and unloved. If, coincidentally, some medical treatment must be given, or if surgery is recommended (tonsillectomy, for example), the child invariably interprets the unpleasant experience as a form of punishment or even of outright dislike on the part of parents or physician.

Small girls of this age who have become aware of the early feelings of excitement in the sex organs sometimes insert crayons, small candles, safety pins, pencils, and other articles into the vagina or rectum. This can lead to damaging psychological results such as morbid shame or feelings of inferiority, unless handled with the greatest tact on the part of both parents and physicians.

The occurrence of a discharge from the vagina is not unusual in the little girl during this period of her sexual development. It does not indicate serious bodily disorder. However, it does mean that the child is under the emotional strain of overexcitement. Sometimes it occurs because of too much fondling or because of an increased desire for intimacy with the parents, for watching them dress and undress, for getting into bed with them, and for increased attention to the body in bathing, toileting, or dressing. This manifestation can best be handled psychologically by making occasion to talk with the child and explaining matters of personal relationship in simple terms that the child can understand.

The case of the small boy is somewhat different. His wishes at this period center largely around the urge to show his prowess in urinating, particularly to his mother. He has frequent erections and is highly aware of sensations in his penis which he wishes to show. Frequent handling and the wish for the mother to help him during urination may become urgent. With the child who has not been circumcised, these actions are often interpreted as evidence of need for circumcision. However, whether or not the operation is indicated, this would be the most unfortunate time for the boy to be subjected to surgical procedure. Every child, boy or girl, undergoing this phase of development should, if possible, be protected from painful medical treatment or surgery.

The attitude of our culture toward sexuality and its development is a strange and negative one. Seldom is sex accorded respect as a basic creative urge and a strong and healthy force in the development of a warm and colorful personality. The concept of sex in the minds of many adults is more definitely related to forms of perversion; these are in reality exaggerated childhood patterns of getting bodily pleasure which, like bodily deformities, are often regarded by these adults as disturbing or disgusting. In the minds of other adults, sex is related to excesses of some kind, such as addictions that come to control the individual and gradually weaken his reason. Because of this attitude the sexual activity of the child is forced into underground channels from which it finally emerges in vulgarity, or in the perverse and infantile activities which society dislikes. It has rarely been accepted as a natural, creative force which contributes not only to successful reproduction, but also in its sublimated forms to social and artistic activity.

The parent who begins at the beginning and gives unembarrassed recognition to the toddler who is discovering his own body and its pleasure feelings avoids the complexity and much of the confusion which must inevitably come when this important first responsibility is overlooked or left to a nurse or playmate. Giving the first and simplest information should definitely be the responsibility of the parents. Questions will be asked by every child whose parents do not have a forbidding attitude, and when the replies are made with frankness and do not go beyond the immediate inquiry, the child is satisfied, and an element of deep trust is added to the parent-child relationship. Sex education is a continuous process up to and through the school age. The endless questions of small children usually stem from unsatisfied curiosity about themselves and their playmates. This curiosity is a highly important stimulus to learning, and through the formulation of questions erotic interest is diverted into learning in other fields.

The common-sense attitude of parents in connection with the erotic impulses of the child is to follow nature's cue and let sex remain latent as far as possible. This does not mean to put pressure on the child, or to forbid his questions or his playfulness with his own body, but rather to avoid exposure to the kind of experiences in family life and among playmates which repeatedly arouse strong curiosity about the body and result in precocious and exaggerated erotic activity.

three

PRIVACY

In the preceding chapter we have attempted to make clear that the component parts of the sex drive are present and active from the time of birth, that a strong charge of sensuous pleasure accompanies the bodily functions of eating and elimination and arouses the earliest mental function of awareness. When these early stages of development are recognized and wisely guided by the parents, a gradual and natural organiza-

tion takes place, flowering briefly in the Oedipus complex. A period of sexual latency follows from roughly
the sixth to the twelfth year.

This natural delay in sex development is characteristic of human beings and is assisted by cultural and
family attitudes. The common-sense point of view for
parents in connection with the sexual feelings of the
child is to follow the cue of natural development and
to avoid as far as possible intimate experiences of
family life which may overstimulate early sensuousness and tend to center the child's interests continu-
ously in his body.

For this reason one of the most urgent needs of
the small child who has begun to walk and talk is a
room of his own. This is a need that is often overlooked
and rarely understood. It is chiefly by means of a good
perspective on early phases of sexual development and
an understanding of the first erotic impulses, soon to
gain momentum, that any sensible estimate can be
made of the real importance of privacy.

A glance back at the first beginnings shows us that
the physical well-being, the organic stability, and the
basic emotional security of a baby are part and parcel
of the closeness and actual physical contact with the
mother. Psychologically, this is a highly creative relationship. The sensuous activities of cuddling, rock-

ing, bathing, and diapering are important stimulants to living in the first months. To the baby this early relationship (to mother or nurse) is in the nature of a sensory awakening, an arousing of the sensitivity of his own body, and probably an important stimulus to the growth and spread of consciousness. Loving and thoughtful parents watch the expansive response which permeates the entire being of the infant as tender loving care and administrations of bodily comfort are given, and they know that all is well.

However, as new faculties toward self-discovery begin to emerge in the child, the way to maturing divides. The urge to move the body about and to become an independent self now partially supplants the earlier sensuous need. The craving for the mother's presence is still intense, her "thereness" is important, so that she can be seen, heard, and called to, but physical contact is no longer so urgent. The child begins to get pleasure in putting his own body into action and in the variety of new experiences that come from independent movement. The vocalizing and babbling mouth activities, accompanied by gesticulation—reaching, playing "pat-a-cake," waving hands—as a means of communication, are maturing into speech which partly takes the place of bodily contact. In order not to prolong the infantile need for frequent cuddling and caressing, or to stimulate new wishes for bodily contact, plans must be made for the personal privacy of the small child.

From the time he can sit up, creep, and play with his first toy, he needs a room of his own for sleeping and for short play periods. If a separate room is not provided until a later stage, removal from the parents' room may be experienced as a rejection. In the meantime, he will soon become overinterested in their undressing, bathing, and toilet activities. The unthinking "sophistication" of some modern parents who sleep without nightwear and go about naked before the small child, bathe with him, sleep with him, is a powerful stimulus to precocious sexual feelings and fantasies which may get out of hand. Hence the need of the child to have a room of his own and to enjoy new play activities which are diverting and help to further sensory interests apart from his body.

This privacy does not mean the sterile isolation which was "fashionable" two or three decades ago, but rather protection from the stimulating effect of too much closeness to adult intimacies. Parents of the last generation, and of the one before that, seem to have had no awareness that the little child has a need for privacy. They were blind to the fact that erotic feelings exist in small children and can be easily aroused by close contact with the sex life of the parents; they steadfastly maintained the theory of "the innocence of childhood."

It was the custom in many families to have a baby share the parents' room, often until he was four or five years of age. When the children came in rapid succession, two or even three children slept in one bed. Often several smaller children occupied the quaint trundle-bed which during the day was shoved under the high four-poster of the parents. It was unthinkable in that era that the child of one or two years could become intensely excited by the physical contact of sleeping in bed with brothers and sisters as well as by the sex life of the parents. Children were supposed to be asleep, "to know nothing of sex," and to pay no attention to sights and sounds connected with parental intercourse. It is true that children do not "know," as does the adult, but they "sense" bodily excitement.

Even today, when the treatment of persons with severe emotional disturbances has repeatedly demonstrated that in childhood these individuals were persistently overstimulated and were sometimes frightened because of their closeness to adult sexual activity, the child's need for privacy is often contested. Many parents find it hard to accept the recommendation that the child of one year should have a room of his own;

it seems to contradict earlier advice to the mother to show constant warmth and affection by cuddling, rocking, and caressing the baby. The modern idea of "rooming in" in maternity hospitals has been instituted so that from the beginning mother and child may be considered as a unit. Some months later this mother is told that separation from the child—if, for example, she goes back to a job—will have an ill effect on the baby; yet here comes a new piece of advice, that the year-old child must have a room of his own and sleep alone.

On the surface, this is somewhat bewildering. To explain the seeming inconsistency, we must return to facts responsible for the child's early sexual and psychological growth. The toddler who has become aware of his own body and the pleasant sensations which accompany many of its activities, and who has a good relationship with the parents, quickly becomes curious about the person of the adult. He observes his parents caressing. He appears suddenly in the bathroom or the shower to look questioningly at various parts of adult anatomy. Creeping into bed with the parents early in the morning is an experience which easily arouses pleasant feelings of excitement in the child.

These interests and activities, though natural and

harmless enough in the beginning, may very quickly become exaggerated to the point of an "addiction." His body responds with erotic excitement. The child is increasingly excited by repeated experiences of physical closeness and begins to watch for occasions when he can indulge them. His sleep may become disturbed and anxiety may be aroused, because his body and mind are not sufficiently developed to cope with this adult kind of excitement and to discharge it. Many parents find it a real sacrifice not to indulge in early morning bed-play. The child gets up early and wants to romp, and it seems a natural sort of activity. However, it is important to romp fully dressed. Another expedient is to place toys or small surprises within reach in the child's own room.

Disastrous results follow when parents intrude their own frustrated needs for physical love into the life of the small child. Without intending it, they arouse physical excitement in him, thereby stimulating latent sex impulses ahead of time.

During the last war when so many fathers left home to enter the army, it became the custom of the lonely mother to have a young child sleep with her. One result of this was that when the father came back, a year or so later, there was set up in the child a violent hostility toward him and a defiant attitude toward the mother. This is equally true of girls and boys. The following story will serve as illustration.

A young physician who had a baby daughter of two years was called to military duty while his wife was early in pregnancy with the second child. He was unable to come home for two years. Some months after he returned to his family, he came to the office of a psychiatrist in serious distress. The sexual behavior of the two little girls was entirely out of control. This had become obvious to the neighbors, who forbade their children to visit his home.

He related, that, when he arrived at home from service, much to his surprise and disappointment neither of the little girls would accept him. The older one, who had slept with her mother, appeared not to remember him and was extremely hostile, so that he was unable to make any sort of a friendly relationship with her.

He noticed that the children seemed particularly curious about his shaving, bathing, and dressing, and he encouraged them to come into the bathroom during these activities with the hope that this might help to restore a close relationship to himself. He also allowed them to come into the shower and bathe with him. Obviously, instead of furthering the father relationship with the little girls, this intensified their difficulties and increased their sexual excitement. The older daughter developed a severe phobia necessitating psychiatric treatment for many months, and the parents sought advice over a long period because of the behavior difficulties of the younger child, who became quite sleepless and required sedation for several weeks.

The same situation occurs obviously in peacetime when a rift in relationship between the mother and father has occurred. One parent becomes overattached to the child and uses him as a solace for loneliness.

The handling of sex problems which have reached such proportions is a long and complicated procedure. Almost inevitably some psychological damage remains, which may seriously distort adolescent development. Troublesome guilt feelings, caused by the child's inability to control precocious sexuality and by his awareness of parental and social disapproval concerning it, makes him an unhappy individual. When the child reaches the stage of walking and talking, the sensible procedure is to avoid excessive physical intimacy between child and parents. Failure to observe this important protective rule may result in later difficulty when the parent is faced with the child's problem of sex play and sex excitement. A state of antagonism may arise between child and parent, accompanied by feelings of guilt on both sides.

It has been consistently found that children between the ages of one and three who sleep in the parents' bedroom and are awake, as they frequently are, when sexual intercourse is going on are stimulated in a way that is damaging to emotional growth. Older children may interpret intercourse as a highly aggressive activity, and feel that they should participate in behalf of the most-loved parent. On the other hand, they may interpret it as a mysterious happening from which they are excluded. Jealousy is aroused, and the feeling of exclusion arouses anxiety. After one or two such experiences, the child becomes wakeful, anticipating repetitions. For the very reason that these adult experiences are so poorly understood by the child, they may assume bizarre forms in his imagination. When he sleeps, he is often awakened by a frightening dream of being smothered and as he gets older these dream experiences become true night-terrors of being gored by a bull or trampled by an elephant.

When sleeplessness and anxiety have taken hold in a young child, it is difficult to uproot them. Usually when these symptoms are present, many other aspects of the child's behavior are disturbed, and smooth psychological development is interrupted. (Problems of elimination frequently arise in this connection.) It is therefore important to prevent overexcitement from the very beginning. This is not to be understood by any means that the child should never see any expressions of warm affection on the part of the parents for each other. When he asks questions as to why he does not sleep with the parents, or with his own brother or sister, it is well to emphasize that his job is growing big and this can happen better if he sleeps alone.

The most serious result of too much petting and other physical contact between the child and the other members of the family is a *fixation* of the early sex impulses to family members. This is true also with regard to other members of the household, nurses or servants. These early seductive experiences are retained persistently in the child's fantasies. At adolescence, when there is a revival of sexual growth, it will be difficult for the young person to throw off these patterns of erotic gratification and turn to people other than his family for emotional and sexual relationships. In this case the natural family ties have been intensified through the early experiences; the possibility of other satisfying relationships is excluded and the young person has an exaggerated family dependency.

The matter of brothers and sisters sleeping together in the same bed at this age as well as at a later age has to be considered. Frequent bodily contact and romping in bed at night or early in the morning have an exciting effect on the child and definitely arouse early sex feelings. Ideally, "a room for every child" is an important family slogan, and when it is recognized as a real need, it can usually be arranged. Practically, modern building materials such as glass bricks can divide a room into two so that a reasonable amount of privacy can be arranged. A room of his own is an important aid in the further sex education of the child and in helping him in self-control.

four

AGGRESSION AND THE MUSCULAR SYSTEM

In a world where aggression in its most crude and cruel forms threatens to dominate the thinking of large social groups and also of national governments, there arises a fresh challenge to explore its roots in human life and its first expression in the early life of the child.

It has long been clear that a period of intense activity, often violent and destructive, emerges in a child in the second year of life. It tends to increase along with muscular development and with the gaining of bodily control. The toddler runs; he rarely walks as locomotion begins. He pushes, snatches, and hits, dramatically sweeping away his dinner dishes as his arm muscles begin to coordinate. When this muscular activity is thwarted, he bites or kicks on what appears to be the mildest provocation.

Parents in different generations have reacted with alarm, bewilderment, or outright annoyance to this type of behavior. In an earlier day they attempted to discipline the two-year-old sternly and rigidly, in the belief that his behavior was evidence of an evil nature; later, they adopted the opposite attitude of complete permissiveness without direction. Neither method has yielded gratifying results.

At the present time we think of aggression in the young child in much the same way that we regard sexuality; as part of a basic biological force related to becoming strong, free, and self-assured, it is energy which is formative and useful. In other words, the expression of aggression in vigorous bodily activity during the second year of life is entirely normal. With the ability to chew, to grasp, to push and pull, to climb and stand, and finally to walk, it is evident that a surge of fresh energy suffuses the entire muscular sys-

tem and makes itself known in no uncertain way in the
toddler. A new kind of pleasure and excitement has
come to him. He is emerging from the passive and helpless stage of infancy into a new phase of life in which
he can do things and go places and be partly self-
directive. He is getting the feel of his body in action.

The aggressive instinct contributes energy to all
kinds of action and effort, destructive and constructive. Hence the cue for parents in handling aggression
at the beginning is to provide for its use in strengthen-
ing the body, gaining freedom of movement, and acquiring skill.

It is important to emphasize and promote the constructive aspects of toddler behavior at this phase of
development. The child is acquiring the use of a basic
functional energy which will contribute to bodily
grace and ease, to free and joyous play, and later to
constructiveness and pleasure in work. Moreover, the
first manipulating of objects—pushing about of small
furniture, and climbing up and down—gives him a
sense of well-being and contributes in this way to
health and growth.

The two-year-old finds important boundaries of self
through his own experimental activities; he discovers
a bit of bodily independence from the mother to do
things and to bring about changes. Much later he will

use some of this executive energy to put thoughts into action.

Parental understanding of the needs of this period and an occasional restrained participation in the child's rowdy activities add greatly to the love feeling of the child for the parents and to his confident acceptance of their moves to divert him to other forms of expression.

Specific needs of this period are in the first place an appropriate playroom or nursery where there are no valuables to be guarded or to be taken away from the child, no treasured books to be pushed down or torn, no delicate clothing to be dragged from bureau or dresser drawers. Rather, this should be a room for many kinds of free activity, furnished with suitable toys such as play chairs and tables, boxes, a set of steps to climb, large light blocks to manipulate, and soft balls which may be thrown. A cabinet for toys with drawers that may be opened and shut with ease is useful, and a set of plastic and unbreakable dishes for lunches are also desirable.

With the acquiring of some independence from the mother, the time will soon come for finding a playmate, especially if there are no brothers and sisters. This first social introduction during the motor aggressive period must be well guarded. The most difficult outbursts to handle are those against a smaller child. Here rapid interference may be necessary, but if it is carried out without alarm or anger the offender will gradually sense the justice of the intervention. He does not yet know the effects of his actions, but as the playmate becomes more valuable the toddler begins to make certain observations: a playmate cries and runs away when he is hit or bitten.

Self-control in the parents is vitally necessary for the successful handling of aggressive activity. Feelings of anger or alarm are quickly communicated to a small child. The parent who has violent or uncontrolled shifts in mood or who is overanxious with regard to what relatives think of him as a parent finds it difficult to direct with wisdom the child's early aggressive behavior and to avoid sudden or angry interference. For this reason careful emotional prophylaxis is helpful in the preparation for psychological parenthood. An occasional temper tantrum in a two-year-old need not be a cause for alarm; he must come to recognize it as a poor solution of his difficulty. In a vigorous child, a tantrum is often the natural expression of too much accumulated frustration and is not harmful. This is equally true of other outbursts, such as violent crying spells, impulsive biting or kicking. To parents these outbursts should indicate a need for new ways of utilizing energy and for more of their own playful participation in the child's activities to make them more satisfying to him. Reassurance for the parent in these situations comes with the knowledge that at this age impulsive actions do not imply serious disturbance but are mainly evidence of immaturity in the child. When met with complete calmness, the tantrum expends itself quickly; on the other hand, when parents betray excitement and uncertainty, the youngster experiences an unhealthy sense of power and is likely to repeat or prolong the outburst.

There is an interesting relationship between walking and muscular control of the body and sphincter control of the bladder and bowels; in each case and in much the same way, the parents must prepare the child to assume direction. An aid to his control of elimination is to provide a small toilet-chair that is comfortable and always available in the nursery when the child is learning to walk, and to offer only friendly and casual suggestions as to its use. Accustoming takes time, and there will of course be many accidents; but this bit of freedom in self-direction has a far-reaching, beneficial effect on the child's personality development. By this easygoing method the average child will soon train himself to daytime evacuations.

During this period of toilet training the child is

peculiarly sensitive, almost as if the products of his body were parts of himself or valued productions. To well-loved parents he presents them as a gift; but toward the parent who is stern and insistent he is likely to become defiant, stubborn, and exhibit strong aggression. The young baby of three or four months can be "conditioned" to eliminate on a small chamber through the local stimulus of applying the buttocks to the vessel at regular intervals. This eases the laundry problem, but does not help the child to direct himself. It has been found conclusively that premature training is merely a reflex action which takes place before control is possible. This early conditioning breaks down in a large percentage of cases, and children so trained frequently become bed-wetters later on. Moreover, children trained early in this way, before body muscles are coordinated under control of the brain, appear to develop tension and are much more aggressive. For this reason it has been found best to wait until the child is walking and beginning to talk before active toilet training is instituted. Soiling as a form of aggression sometimes occurs when a child has been trained too fast or too vigorously and has not been allowed to take part in his own training. It is not difficult with clear understanding to make this aspect of bodily control a largely self-directed activity.

Apart from the question of muscular development and control the most important factor in this early training is again the relationship to the trainers, that is, the parents. If this is a happy one, and the training is a true education and not a rigid discipline, the successful establishment of cleanliness progresses easily.

It is an interesting fact that young animals—kittens, puppies, calves, and colts—have good motor coordination and play vigorously in the first weeks of life. Their energies are quickly channeled into body-moving activities. The human child, on the other hand, is for many months passively sensing and registering in his developing brain the parent activities that are contributing to his well-being. His perceptive faculties develop in advance of his muscular functions and in his gaining dominance over them. This gives him the advantage of being able to accept direction from his parents and gradually to assume muscular control. He is thus equipped to function most effectively and happily in relation to another person. He is going to be predominantly a social being. With the development of speech his higher brain functions come into action and by this means he becomes able to enjoy social activity as well as crude self-assertion.

After the child has learned to talk well, he has an additional way of expressing himself, and the method of controlling aggression changes somewhat. The parent is able to point out quietly and without blame the effects, for example, of aggressive attacks on another child. It is possible by "talking it over" to demonstrate the pleasure gain of positive play activities and of companionship with siblings or playmates and the advantages of social behavior over crude aggression.

Real teaching begins at this point, but it must be tactful, slow, and not too insistent. It is helpful to tell a brief story occasionally in the child's terms, with simple illustrations, of the effects of hurting another child. First comes a long period of acting freely and sensing some of the effects of ruthlessness (a broken toy, a playmate who cries and runs away because he was hit or bitten, or perchance a pet animal who scratches back after being patient too long). Gradually the child comes to understand the results of aggressive behavior and to think before he acts.

The outstanding aggressive personality trait of the toddler is possessiveness. This trait has deep roots in the relationship between infant and mother. The close unity of the first months of life gives the child the impression that mother is a part of himself. The discovery of his own body and his power to initiate its function is a very gradual process. Actual awareness of the mother as a separate individual begins with locomotion. However, mother still belongs to him. Full recognition starts only after self-awareness has become well established. For these reasons separations from the mother in the first and second years are painful; the child is developing functionally *by means of* the relationship with her and the bodily care she gives. Having to wait for her return or to wait for his food is a strain which makes him demanding and later on aggressive. This is a biological situation arising from incompleteness and the intense needs of the rapidly growing body and brain; it is not a situation in which he will learn endurance. The child does not yet *know* that hunger pains will not destroy him, nor is he sure that his mother will return.

These discoveries of self and mother are a natural part of maturing, but if forced on the child prematurely, he tends to feel threatened and to cling. This is particularly true in children who have been abruptly or unskillfully weaned. Sudden or too early removal from the breast causes every normal infant to become uneasy and gradually more possessive, and to cling to the mother with an unhealthy intensity.

The sense of belonging is important to the toddler at the time that he is gaining independence. He must have his own time to achieve a new form of security within himself, to become "self-possessed." As new capacities develop the child gets a sense of gaining new parts of himself. Acquisitiveness has a biological implication. New objects that he discovers and all new toys are "his," even though they may belong to another child. He is indeed "grasping," but it must be remembered that he is living through the process of completing himself.

Furthermore, whatever he grasps goes into his mouth, as though he would eat up his possessions and thus incorporate them. This gives us a clue to the fact that the traits of early possessiveness and grasping are rooted in food hunger as well as incompleteness. Oral activity, which was very recently the center of his being and brought such intense pleasure, knows no discrimination as yet, and the process of "incorporation" is still vigorously at work. For example, a young child taken to a beach will joyfully ingest sand until someone interferes, although his activity will bring on a serious attack of diarrhea and yield no possible pleasure except from the recent association of hand-to-mouth pleasure.

Prophylaxis against aggressiveness can begin in the first year of life, permitting the infant complete freedom of sucking activities and frequent hunger satisfaction. It is necessary to make generous provision for biting activity while the teeth are developing and chewing movements are in evidence. The introduction of self-feeding and of new foods very slowly at the appropriate time will aid greatly in avoiding oral demandingness. Allowing free bodily movement, preferably without clothing, once or twice during the day has been found to bring release of muscular tension. Hand activity with toys and free creeping and climbing promotes the useful expression of nascent motor aggressiveness. These simple procedures tend to direct aggressive energy into functional channels which are useful, whereas any form of muscular restraint is known to foster aggressiveness.

With a better understanding of the roots of possessiveness it is easy to draw the conclusion that its cousin, jealousy, follows a similar course. It may be aroused early in the child's life by factors in the relationship between the parents. An unstable father who wishes to have his wife to himself and regards the child as an intruder may show his feelings in ways that frighten the child and increase his possessive feeling toward the mother; an unstable mother may bring about the same result. The increased possessiveness toward parents may take the form of extreme hyperactivity and aggression.

It is a fairly common situation, particularly with a first child, that father and mother become rivals for the child's affections. The psychological effects of this are extremely bad. It is easy for the child to react in opposite directions so that love goes to one parent and hatred to the other. When a shift comes about and the loved parent becomes the hated one, these first personal ties are weakened.

The jealousy which invariably develops when the next sibling is born is also more understandable from the point of view of the child's feelings of possessiveness for the mother. On her part, a transfer of feeling from the older child to the coming one is natural and for the most part unconscious; but the child of two years has little ability to transfer his feelings of possessiveness. Even with the most loving discussion of the coming baby, the toddler is unable to grasp what is happening until he sees the new infant in the mother's arms. Then he is overwhelmed by the feeling that he is entirely dispossessed; his rage and disappointment are quite likely to find expression in aggression.

There are, of course, highly destructive aspects in the aggression of the two-year-old. He gets a thrill of power from breaking what is fragile, from teasing animals, from stepping on bugs, and from making the baby cry. Can these tendencies be handled successfully by providing in advance suitable outlets for the child's energy? Is it possible to avoid occasions which arouse excessive and destructive aggression? The answer is "Yes" for the average child whose parents have understanding and have developed skill in avoiding frustrating situations and in diverting his outbursts of rage. This good relationship to the parents can support the child through the difficult period of his early aggressiveness.

A distressed father reported an incident which convinced him that his small son, aged two and a half, had "something vicious" in his make-up. There were two other children in the family, a sister, Mary (a little older than the boy), and a baby two months old. On the day the incident occurred the father was working in the garden, and the little boy was helping the father by hauling away stones in his toy wagon. The child seemed uneasy and suddenly rushed into the house to find his mother. A few minutes later he returned, hesitated a moment, then picked up a piece of iron pipe lying on the ground and started toward his sister who was peacefully playing with her doll. The obvious intent was to hit her over the head with the pipe. The father was barely able to prevent serious injury to the unsuspecting little girl. What did you do? he was asked. "I yelled at him, 'Johnny, drop the pipe!' and hurried to the rescue. Then I took him into the house and whaled him soundly, after which I asked him, 'Would you like for Daddy to hit you with that piece of pipe?' " There was no answer, and the child lay on his bed sobbing for a long while before he fell asleep.

We asked this parent whether whipping a small child will teach him not to "hit," and whether brain rather than brawn could not be used more effectively to teach him. Without inquiring into possible causes for the incident the father was viewing it with all the seriousness and alarm that he might feel if Johnny were ten years old and had shown deliberate intentions of murdering his sister. After careful questioning of both parents as to events immediately preceding the "unprovoked attack" the mother related the following: she was rocking the baby to sleep when Johnny burst into the room calling her loudly. She hushed him up and pushed him impatiently aside, telling him to go into the yard and play with his sister. In the yard he found Mary busily undressing her doll. It is evident that to the unhappy little boy this represented his mother giving his place to the new baby and his immediate impulse was to get rid of the painful situation.

These parents, though highly intelligent and certainly not intentionally cruel, were quite unaware of the latent aggressive urges natural to Johnny's age and of the intense jealousy the child would feel for the new baby. Nor did they know that reasoning is weak at this age and has to be put to use with the help of wise and knowing parents, and that aggression is an intense instinctive urge which, during the period from one and a half to three years, unless carefully deflected, sweeps all before it.

It must be remembered that the child who has suffered from physical illness or surgery requires more affection and more time to grow up. During convalescence, protest accumulates in the child; he is unable to understand the reasons for his pain, hence he needs help in mastering the aggression that is a natural reaction to a disagreeable experience.

Parents who accept the theory that the aggressive activities of the two-year-old represent an expression of important life energy, which is charging the motor system and contributing to self-development and ultimate constructiveness, will readily see that punishment is inappropriate and that rigid restriction is useless because it only increases what it seeks to curb. The logical aim of parents then is to divert this energy into functional expression for later use in mastering difficult situations, in self-defense, in competition, and especially in the pursuit of knowledge. True mastery of aggressive impulses and more consistent substitution of social gains comes two or three years later with the development of reasoning and with more experience in living.

The child who is left undirected by the completely permissive parent is more disconcerted by the license that is allowed him than by the restrictions imposed on him. Unlimited and aimless permissiveness is not freedom for the child. Actually it interferes seriously with the course of his development, and as a result aggression continues with increasing vigor into the third and fourth years of life. By this time the child is seriously unhappy, because he is thoroughly disliked by members of his family and other adults and finds himself unable to win friends of his own age or to get along in a group.

five

THE BEGINNINGS OF SELF

Self-awareness and the capacity for self-observation as it emerges in the young child is one of the most interesting phases of psychological development. It marks the beginning of a form of mental life more like that of the adult and indicates definite progress on the road to maturing. Yet strangely enough this definite advance in mental growth with its important implications is often overlooked.

Parents have become so engrossed in the theory of giving the instincts free rein in order to avoid crippling them by repression that they have neglected the growth and early expressions of the ego. Others have associated self and its activities predominantly with the moral concept of selfishness as it appears in the older child and the adult, and this misconception may be responsible for their neglect of the child's urges toward self-building.

Me feelings and eagerness to participate become evident about the time the child can walk, can gesticulate his wishes vigorously, and has acquired a small vocabulary that delights his parents. The all-important discovery that his body belongs to him and that he can initiate many of its activities adds a new glow of knowingness. He has become a person. "Me do it" now becomes insistent. Self-knowledge leads to clearer awareness of other selves—of parents as more distinct persons. It paves the way for better self-direction and for making choices in the course of action. Later on it will lead to recognition of cause and effect and to discrimination between what is real and what is make-believe.

A mother made a good observation in an enthusiastic report to me of her small daughter's progress. The report serves to make vivid the changes in a young child's psychological reactions while self-feeling was emerging during the latter half of the second year. On her first birthday, Joan exhibited little interest in the many toys given her by family and friends, much to the disappointment of those who were present for the birthday celebration. They had spent time selecting things considered appropriate and were quite downcast when after a casual glance the youngster ignored their gifts and clung to a battered and much-chewed plastic doll, her first plaything. At one year, attention was centered in the mouth and what went into it, and interest was absorbed in moving her own body.

Ten months later her father, to whom she was strongly attached, brought her one evening a fluffy waddling duck, her first mechanical toy. Joan beamed with pleasure as she pressed the downy plaything to her face. Her father took it from her, and she held out her hands impatiently as he wound it up and placed it on the floor in front of her. As it began to move she hesitated for an instant, then scrambled to her feet and "waddled" cautiously along with the toy. A door was open across the room in the direction toward which child and toy were moving. Suddenly the little one left her duck and darted over to push the door violently shut.

The mother realized that this sequence represented

Joan's complete direction of attention to the new toy, her wish to possess it and to make it part of herself.

In the all-important ten months since her first birthday, Joan's self-security had developed and her mental reactions had advanced to a remarkable degree. She could walk securely and could therefore identify herself with moving objects. She was ready to participate in a new adventure. A new toy was no longer something entirely strange—she had seen pictures of animals and birds and could now relate the duck to her own locomotion. Finally, memory and experience told her that an open door meant disappearance, which she did not like; so by her own reasoning and action she prevented the disappearance of a delightful toy.

Self-feeling is a composite, as we have already seen, of many different bodily sensations and numerous sorts of experience. Some of the contributing factors are the first using together of mouth, eyes, and hands; self-feeding; and body sensations of touch that occur during bathing and when clothing is put on and off. Gaining muscular control of the body—lifting the head, sitting, standing, creeping, and walking—advances self-feeling still further. The control of elimination is an extremely important part of this early self-direction, this progress. Self-expression in speech is a climax in mental growth and personal relatedness which brings with it a vigorous advance in self-awareness.

The mental self or ego is a mirror image, a dynamic replica of the bodily self. In addition to his observations of himself, the child now knows that his mother and father are two different sorts of persons. During the process of gaining bowel and bladder control, the child inevitably makes direct observations of other children and of animals, so that he has already become aware of the differences in bodily structures. Still earlier he has sensed the fact that his mother's breast, with its softness and warmth, is not the same as the firmness and solidity of his father and that parents meet his various needs in different ways. (This is one reason why the participation of father in early care is of basic importance.)

To this early knowledge there is added a new set of facts through the child's own body. Sexual organization is now well under way and sensuous feeling is becoming centered in the sex organs. Some youngsters fantasy vividly at this time that there is only one sex, that mother has male organs and father has an invisible breast. Others need to believe that they themselves can be both sexes. Not being identical with both parents is a difficult idea to tolerate because it implies some defect in the child himself. At this time, whenever the occasion arises, the youngster needs the assurance that it is good to be a boy like daddy or a girl like mommie.

Fantasies of this kind occur more often in children whose parents do not have a full, mature relationship with one another. These children, never having gained the impression that father and mother complete each other and need each other, find it difficult to adopt the role of the parent of the same sex. From time to time the child impersonates the activities of his father and his mother in an experimental way. On the other hand, the effects of his own behavior on mother and father become much clearer to him and he senses keenly what pleases them. Father plays an increasingly important role at this time, particularly if he has taken part in the early care of the child. The fact that he comes and goes in a way mysterious to the child becomes increasingly interesting. This distinguishes him from mother, who stays near at hand.

The young self urgently needs recognition and support from both parents in order to grow progressively in greater independence and in self-understanding. The child needs particularly to be taken seriously and not laughed at, even when his thinking is highly colored with fantasy. He is already a more rational individual, but it must be remembered that his systems of control are just beginning to come into action and that there will be many outbursts of jealousy, greed, and possessiveness which are still a natural part of his behavior. They will lessen, however, as the self grows stronger and more assured.

"Conflict" has already arisen in his young life between the urge to assert himself and the wish to be loved and admired. Opportunities for solving the conflict and for learning to make a good decision must be provided, because this is an important means of furthering ego development and stimulating the growth of intelligence. The important factor is free self-expression and freedom to develop the ability to think for himself. The utmost tact and restraint are needed by the parents. Enthusiastic approval of the wise choice is in order, but strong disapproval or the resort to coercion by father or mother tends to weaken the child's ability to make a decision. Parents must convince themselves that poor solutions of conflict at this age are at many times inevitable and are a part of immaturity.

This leads us to consider the characteristic human potentiality for what is known as *sublimation*. This capacity is present in the earliest stages of ego development and grows with use and exercise. Fundamentally, it means the deflection of energy from crude instinctual expression to wider functional uses of body and mind and to varied forms of gratification. In the previous stage of development it was necessary for the parents to act for the child and divert impulses which were strongly aggressive or too persistently sexual. However, with the growing sense of self the child begins to discover that he can substitute other interests if the relationship to the parents is warm, sympathetic, and approving. Hence disappointment is not overwhelming. The urge for pleasure still dominates him in this period of life, but if he has become aware of social pleasure and of the satisfaction of praise from his parents, the process of sublimation is not too difficult. It is necessary that parents help to make the new gain of emotional satisfaction greater for the child than were the earlier infantile pleasures.

A new enjoyment comes with the ability to talk well. To the parents, speech indicates that a learning faculty is at work. The royal road to learning and ego building in this period is through talking, and the important role of the parents is that of making opportunities "to talk things over." It is best if this comes about quietly and casually, the mother sitting by with handwork or looking at a magazine, or the father perhaps demonstrating a new toy. Talking comes most readily after a period of vigorous exercise or of play activity. Unfortunately many parents, not recognizing its value for the child, are annoyed by persistent talking or questioning; this is especially true of fathers who have had a busy day at the office and to whom the child's chatter may be highly disturbing. Often the child is told to be quiet, or to run away and play.

Forbidding him to talk is plainly a serious restriction. This does not mean, however, that the family mealtime should be spoiled and that family privacy and social visits should be interfered with. It does mean that the child must be provided with frequent occasions to talk freely and play spontaneously with parents, siblings, or visitors. Meals taken in the company of mother or nurse, and very occasionally with a playmate, are an advantage when, during the first three years, attention remains on the food and its handling rather than on conversation. This helps to avoid many eating difficulties and protects the family mealtime.

Why is talking such an important means of ego building? The answer lies in the child's developmental history. The mouth, we will remember, is the first equipment of the baby which is ready to go into action at birth. Sucking is the first source of pleasure. The mouth retains this strong pleasure association. Through babbling and vocalization it gradually becomes the organ of speech. In this way early oral gratification lends some of its drive to the mental activity of formulating words, and some of the early pleasure associated with mouth activity and eating is transferred to the social satisfaction of talking.

An example observed by the writer at a social gathering at the home of a close friend gives the best clarification of the thinking of a boy two and a half years old whose mind is groping for answers to the situation of a new baby sister who is breast-fed by his mother. Climbing out of his crib he slips into the living room where a group of his mother's friends have assembled for a dinner party. He goes directly to a motherly, well-bosomed lady, climbs into her lap, and talks out his problem in conversation: patting her bosom he asks tensely, "You got a baby?"

"No, dear, my babies have all grown up to be big people." Insistently patting the breast of the lady who is giving him her full attention, he inquires further, "What you got here?" The wise woman hesitates a moment then replies, "That's a pillow for a little child to rest his head on when he is going to sleep."

Evident relief is seen in the youngster, who leans his head comfortably against his friend. He is understood and his questions answered. But there are titters of laughter across the room. Sliding to the floor the small boy takes the hand of his friend and leads her into his nursery, where he serenely goes back to bed.

With a total lack of comprehension of what has occurred in the mind of the child, the lady who has laughed nervously says, "They begin early, don't they?" To which her neighbor replies, "He'll be a fresh one in a few years." They missed the point that question and answer were more important to the child and that he was fortunate in having someone to whom he could talk, someone who could answer not only his questions but also the disturbing situation that prompted them.

In this same way the child is stimulated to express his fantasies to the trusted parent. These fantasies are usually startling to the adult, but the very expression of them helps the child to correct the unreality of some of his first thinking. The early thinking revolves around himself and his bodily experiences of pleasure and pain. Pleasurable experiences are retained, and from disagreeable happenings his awareness tends to withdraw. This makes many of his expressions seem strange to his parents and gives an impression of falseness, but, again, talking about them—giving expression to them—is vital to the learning of reality.

As long as the wishes of parents are not in too great

conflict with the child's erotic feelings and aggressive pleasures, the formulations which he has made in fantasy and has come to express in speech will gradually be revised by his own growing critical faculties.

This first learning of the child cannot be a set or routine procedure; it should not depend on schedule or on the mood of the parents, but rather on the cue of readiness and responsiveness in the child. When these early stages of education are made pleasurable and dramatic and stimulating, the learning which begins to feed the mind becomes highly desirable to the child. He gets definite satisfaction from knowing things and "feeding his ego." In this way learning can tend to become as spontaneous and gratifying as eating.

If we consider speech from another angle it will serve to make clear some of the personal factors in the relationship between child and parent which may inhibit or damage this basic function of intercommunication and ego expression.

A little girl of six years was brought for psychological help because she had entirely lost the ability to speak on two occasions, and for more than a year had refused to say a word to anyone outside her immediate family. Even at home she often spoke in a whisper, and it was almost impossible to understand her. As is usually the case, not one but many traumatic experiences contributed to the functional disturbance. The father, a dignified and highly intelligent clergyman, said that Janet's difficulty had begun more than two years earlier when her new brother was born. It had been arranged that an aunt would come to stay with Janet and her older sister while the mother was in the hospital giving birth, but because of the aunt's illness the plan had to be changed suddenly. Without previous explanation the children were placed in a good nursery. They were told briefly that their mother was going away to get a new baby and that they would stay in the nursery until she came back. From the first, Janet refused to play or talk, even with her sister. She also refused to eat, so that after two days she was forcibly fed.

Convinced that the child must be seriously ill, the director advised Janet's father to take her to a nearby children's hospital for examination. Here also she refused to speak or eat and was finally fed through a tube introduced into her stomach. No organic cause could be discovered to account for her negative and withdrawn attitude.

On returning home, Janet spoke very little and always in a whisper. She refused to look at the baby brother and was highly antagonistic to her mother. The eating difficulties continued intermittently, though gradually her condition improved at home. Her dislike of the baby remained intense and the parents decided to place her in kindergarten the following fall (Janet was then four and a half). The first day in school she reverted to whispering. Great effort was made by the teachers (who knew the parents well and were very eager to help the child), but she did not respond, and after some weeks in which she became progressively more withdrawn, she was taken out of school.

Medical help was again sought and every known test was made to determine any possible organic cause of the disturbance. The father consulted speech specialists, neurologists, pediatricians, and finally sought psychological help.

When asked about Janet's early development the father became decidedly uneasy. "To tell the truth, we did not want this child, and she has been a burden since the day she was born." She cried most of the time for the first eight months of her life. Finally, in a desperate effort to stop the crying, the father decided to sit by the baby and cry when she did, only louder! Sometimes this worked, but after someone came in from the street to see what was the matter the method was abandoned. "Evidently it had some effect," the father said, "because afterward a slight tap on the lips would quiet her."

After this embarrassing confession was made, Janet's mother took up the story of the child's development. The parents were on a long-anticipated holiday in Europe when her pregnancy of three months was discovered. The trip was curtailed. Despite several attempts to "get rid of" the foetus, a lusty little girl was born—the father had been eager for a son. For six weeks the child was breast-fed and then abruptly weaned because the mother became tense over her increasing responsibilities. She "lost her milk," and the baby was not gaining weight. Janet resisted bottle-feeding. In the mother's words, "She lost all appetite, though she began to cry incessantly as if hungry." The parents adopted the "leave the child alone" method which was in vogue at the time, and they did not hold her or play with her or attempt to comfort her. Muscularly she developed slowly and could not sit up at seven months. "She was like a rag doll."

A pediatrician was consulted because of the child's poor muscular development. He found no organic trouble but something prompted him to ask the mother "Do you love this child, and show her some attention?" The uneasy and guilt-laden mother began then to shower attention on the little one who for some time "literally blossomed." She began to talk at sixteen months and progress in speech development continued until she contracted whooping cough at twenty-six months. At this time again Janet was given much attention by both parents, who feared that she might die in the violent attacks of coughing.

The child's speech difficulty was cured after many months of psychological treatment but it soon became evident that this was not her only problem. This unhappy little girl had developed distorted emotional attitudes toward her entire family. Toward the mother who brought her to me daily for therapy she was at times clinging and dependent but often openly defiant. Toward her father she later revealed fear which impelled her to be good in his presence but in her over-developed fantasy life he was a cruel and threatening giant. Toward her sister she was sometimes highly aggressive, biting, scratching and deliberately destroying her belongings, and at other times crudely loving, attempting to kiss her over the entire body, or showing her a cloying sweetness and attention. These family relationships improved to some extent during her treatment, and the parents were able with much help to understand some of the emotional factors which had entered into the child's illness.

We can understand in Janet's case how the emotional coldness of her parents and their lack of consistency contributed to her speech disturbance. Sensitized by painful infant experiences, she interpreted the birth of the brother as meaning that she was no longer wanted. But evidently in back of her emotional disturbance was a functional difficulty with respiration which had affected the early elements of speech. She had been breast-fed for six weeks, then abruptly weaned by her highly unstable mother. The insistent crying which followed over a period of six months indicates some physiological difficulty with respiration which is sometimes seen in young infants who are suddenly weaned and who have insufficient stimulus from parental care. The strange attempts of her father to stop the crying added an additional injury. Aided by her mother's lavish affection, her growth was stabilized and she made good progress, thus showing an essentially good organic and nervous constitution. Whooping cough followed, a serious illness in the first part of life. Respiration was again threatened.

In the first six months the component parts of speech are predominantly organic (somatic) rather than psychic. The baby whose respiration is well established instead of crying persistently begins to babble and gurgle, thus exercising his vocal chords and also producing vibratory sounds that stimulate his hearing. When in addition parents sing and talk to him, his development is furthered at this time, emotional responses are elicited, and later on an urge to communicate develops. Little by little the expressionless mask-like face of the young infant who is loved becomes a responsive face breaking into smiles of recognition of parental speech and attention. (Janet never smiled.) Thus psyche and soma develop hand in hand and the basic incentive to both is a pleasant relatedness to parents who bring comfort and relieve inner tensions. Speech, of course, develops automatically through the energy of the growth process within the brain. However, this highly social function may be inhibited by parental rejection just as it can be furthered immeasurably by warmth and understanding. Janet had basically a good mind which responded to treatment and resumed its growth. In the years since her treatment she has graduated from high school with honors. The question remains open however whether she does not carry with her a damaged *self* which under outward stress can again break down.

Play activity is a valuable way of developing the early ego functions. Games initiated by the child himself, at times in a group, are particularly valuable. Respect for his play activity contributes greatly to the child's relationship to the parents at this point. The play theme can be furthered and carried along as a story; play is a serious and engrossing matter during this period of life. A well-arranged and well-equipped playroom is the child's workshop, where he gets a sense of his own possessions and where his deepest interests can be dramatized. Sudden interruption of this play by a mealtime or need for a rest period is disconcerting. It is well for the parents to think ahead so that an easy transition can be made.

The instant compliance required by the old school of parental authority has been definitely found to produce defiance and rebellion in a healthy child, whereas in the passive dependent type of youngster it deepens the dependency. Fortunately, abrupt demands on a three-year-old are nowadays chiefly limited to extreme emergency, for example, when the child is in danger. Frequent requests for cooperation from a four-year-old must also be made with tact and with consideration for the complete understanding of the child. The youngster is mentally occupied in learning self-protection, self-control, and the niceties of group behavior, as well as in many other psychological adjustments within himself. The wise parent who realizes the child's preoccupation at this stage will not insist upon immediate compliance to a request or a demand.

It is often a great surprise to parents to find that the child loses hold of or abandons some of his ego functions when his mother is not there "to keep up his morale." This does not mean that she has to act for him, but rather that she answers a certain need for reassurance. Sometimes highly efficient or overprotective parents function so completely for the child that his self-development is slowed up and he becomes too dependent. He is still fed by mother at the age of two because "he messes with his food"; he is not encouraged to dress himself because "it takes too long"; or he does not participate in putting away his toys because no one "has the time" to do it with him regularly and to give the process a dramatic incentive.

Providing imaginative conversation, a song, or even a record appropriate to each period of development is a helpful part of making orderliness pleasurable. There are also times when a nurse finds it much easier and quicker to do everything for the child rather than to let him participate. A bodily sickness or a hospital experience retards the course of self-development, because in these instances complete care of all personal needs is taken over by mother or nurse.

Relapses into dependency must be noted, so that quick recovery may take place and the temporary loss of self-function may not become a persistent weakness. A vigorous child quickly recovers his functional losses. Yet if several setbacks occur, and if they are complicated by such things as previous change in the nursing personnel, long absences of the parents, or strong inconsistencies in parental care, a serious tendency to regress may be set in motion. Energy is then withdrawn from the developmental process and is automatically turned backward to reanimate the earliest infantile functions.

This halting or turning back in self-development, which especially at this age is so closely related to physical illness or disfunction or to the birth of a sibling, is a serious matter. It is most apt to occur early in the third year of life and its onset may be difficult to recognize. It assumes many forms in the child's behavior which often are mistaken for naughtiness. There may be refusal to adjust to familiar routine, and eating and sleeping habits are likely to be upset. The child of three or four may begin to suck his thumb and become so withdrawn in fantasy that he does not respond at once when parents or playmates talk with him. It is highly unfortunate when this regressive process is mistaken for bad behavior and punished, or when attempts are made to deal with it without first finding the sources of the disturbance. If physical illness has been the cause, the process of convalescence and of restoring energy to the activities of maturing will require a great deal of wisdom on the part of the parents. Some of the old "babying" may be necessary, along with frequent assurances of affection. The control of elimination is frequently lost during a physical illness and its reacquisition may be a tedious process. It is necessary to go over the same ground in restoring control and to avoid all impatience and disapproval. With good understanding of this regressive process, complete recovery can usually be established, and as a rule no permanent damage is done to the development itself.

It is well to remember that hand activity and speech are major tools for ego expression and that serious injury can be done by restricting them before understanding is well developed and the youngster can use some voluntary control. Slapping mischievous hands or forbidding a young child to touch his sex organs or to play with his body is unwise. The hands must be playfully and gently redirected to some other form of activity, so that no inhibiting association may later affect the acquiring of such skills as writing and drawing.

six

LOVE AND HATE

⌣ The emotion of love grows in a child in response to the constant affection of parents who understand him, accept him as he is, and guide him from one phase of maturing to the next. Love is a powerful factor in personality development. It helps to deflect energy from crude instinctual aims into the wider areas of pleasure to be gained from companionship in family life and with playmates. On the other hand, feelings of tension, aroused by lack of understanding or by subtle hostility and dislike, mount steadily into hate and protest against the entire process of acculturation.

Antagonism, once aroused, tends to increase with each phase of development, so long as force, coercion, or punishment is used in place of guidance. When negative, antagonistic responses appear, a prompt and searching investigation into the cause is important. Frequently such responses indicate that parents are too serious and determined in such matters as conformity to schedule, or that they have lost in adult life the quality of playfulness so necessary for communicating affection to a small child. Perhaps they never elicit smiles and laughter and seldom rock and sing the child to sleep. Affection, which is life-giving for the infant, is also essential to the toddler. It plays an actively curative role in his problems of grief, pain, and anger. The solution of these tensions usually lies in some appropriate way of showing affection which the youngster can understand.

The groundwork for emotional development is laid in the first year of life. Babies are born with some capacity to respond positively to another human being. After the first week of life an infant fixes his gaze on the human face that approaches him, but not on any inanimate object. At four or five weeks the look is often followed by a smile and a gurgle. The hands of the child grope toward the feeder during the meal, and by four or five months there is definite recognition of a familiar face. A charge of excitement through the entire muscular system accompanies the smile of greeting. From this time on, definite seeking and reaching toward the most familiar parent is seen. A basic relationship has been established. At this tender age it is not clearly love, but rather an expansive reaction to the satisfaction of need, a reaction which paves the way to loving—and also to the functions of perception and recognition.

An important way in which positive feeling reactions are stimulated in the child is in the care of his body. This includes feeding, bathing, dressing, and arrangements for sleeping periods. Here the parent naturally takes the active role. The skill and tenderness with which these activities are carried out contribute toward the child's first love feeling toward other persons who bring comfort and pleasure. This early care becomes to the small child a relational experience of great importance, even though to the busy parent it may soon become routine and perfunctory.

At the age of two, most children are able to put on socks, use the wash cloth vigorously, and cooperate in other matters of the toilet, even though they have lit-

tle awareness of the purpose of these activities. However, if the parent is suddenly called to the telephone
the entire procedure stops, because for the child a
pleasant companionable experience has been interrupted. Resourceful parents will think up new ways of
introducing substitute satisfactions in simple domestic
projects in which mutual participation can be enjoyed
and in which companionship is emphasized predominantly; otherwise it will be difficult later to shift
dressing activity to the status of an objective accomplishment. Even in the fourth year when the child can
do a creditable job of dressing himself there may be
great sensitiveness and hurt feelings if no help is given.
The child's ego is slow to take over this maintenance
program until his emotional needs are satisfied in other
ways.

Parents easily become exasperated by this type of
dependency and a gradual nagging develops: "Be a
good girl and put on your shoes"; "Be a good boy and
wash your face." Often there is no response, because
the child's feelings are hurt, his attention is withdrawn, and he has resorted to fantasy. Then come
threats and sometimes actual punishment. "The child
is unreasonable," protest the parents. Yes, this behavior
is not reasonable but emotional, and emotional growth
can be seriously disturbed by seemingly trivial mat-

ters. Needs for love have to be satisfied. Here parents need leisure and freedom from haste in order to devise ways and occasions for answering this need. Otherwise antagonism develops on both sides.

It is difficult for young children to understand love in the abstract. They have little ability to recognize the continuous thought and planning of their parents. Often adults remark how little they appreciated the consistent care given them as children until they themselves became parents. It is concrete attention which stimulates a love response and this kind of care is of the greatest importance. Fathers who put a "bond a month" in the bank for the child's future education may dimly expect gratitude of which the child is not capable. But the toddler will respond joyfully to a romp before dinner, the three-year-old to an interesting story told or read before bedtime, and youngsters of any age to a family project such as building a doll's house, a dog kennel, or some play benches.

When mother says "I am tired now and must rest a little," or, "Can't you see that I am busy?" she must ask herself whether the child understands her meaning and *can* give this cooperation. He does not know of her selflessness in giving up a trip or a fur coat in order to pay the maid to attend to household routine so that she will have time enough to devote to projects with him. Yet love responses must be brought out. This is not "spoiling" as some educators think. It is regard for progressive development of emotional health.

The toddler's love response to his parents is spontaneous and altogether charming but is of brief duration. Within a few minutes after a display of affection he may feel hatred that is intense and inclines him—unless he has been intimidated—to strike out, to bite, or to throw whatever is in his hand. His feelings, like his attention, are extremely distractable. He is involved at this age in enjoying himself, in trying out new play activities and keeping on the move. If he is hurt, he will run back to his parents for comfort and expressions of love. Chiefly he is fascinated by his discovery of strong feelings within his own person; in other words, he loves himself.

Parents are often disappointed, even resentful, because of this fickleness and inconstancy in the child and because of his readiness to hate. They overlook the fact that emotions like other mental qualities mature slowly and that the relationship on the part of the child is still one in which dependency predominates. Yet emotional growth comes by means of these swings from love to hate. The toddler is incapable of constancy in his affections, and his chief response to good parental care is shown in growing alertness and progressive healthy maturing. His loyalty will come when he is more sure of himself and is able to think with ease and understand meanings.

For this reason parents need a strong love for each other if the trinity, father-mother-child, is to grow on a positive emotional basis. They must be content for a time with their own creativeness and must continue to fulfill the intense emotional needs inherent in the self-completion of the child.

The toddler soon senses the enthusiastic response in his parents to an embrace, a kiss, or any friendly overture. He may use it to wheedle indulgences for himself. In this way he can become "spoiled"—in other words, his parents have missed the cue for diverting satisfactions from one area to another, with the result that balance is lost. Frequent overindulgence invariably leads to trouble in the child's distribution of energy.

The emotions of the three-year-old are highly possessive and demanding; they are also highly charged with erotic feeling. Often he likes to kiss and cuddle, exhibiting a need for physical closeness. He has curiosity about the bodily functions of adults. His reactions of love and hate are stronger than those of the toddler and last longer.

At the age of four the child begins to single out the parent of the opposite sex for the increased expressions of love. The boy becomes protective of his mother and wants much personal attention from her and at the same time becomes antagonistic to his father. The girl seeks increased affection from her father and begins to feel that her mother is a rival for her father's love. This is an important and also a difficult phase of emotional growth, and expert help is needed from both parents.

It is a great achievement in the mental life of the five-year-old when he becomes able to restrain some of his aggressiveness and his sexual urges and can love both parents, as well as other members of the family, without the violence and impulsiveness which were a part of the earlier years. Being able to express emotion in word and action without loss of control constantly tests the strength of his ego. Success depends largely on the attitude of parents, on their deep love for each other, and on the understanding that they have shown through the early stages of the child's development.

Strange though it may seem, hate is a necessary emotion in the life of human beings. It is an offspring of aggression and arises as a primitive form of self-defense and of maintaining freedom. We have seen in a previous chapter how closely aggression is related to the development of muscular strength and ability and how it contributes to bodily control and to early independence. The first sense of freedom comes to a small child as he emerges from the complete helplessness of infancy and becomes able to move his own body about. From this freedom he acquires a fundamental sense of self which seems to initiate an impulse toward self-defense. Being compelled to sit still at the age of two is an infringement on this first natural sense of freedom and arouses protest which sometimes develops into a fight. We have seen that, a little earlier in his development, biting also gives the child a sense of strength and power. Unless he has been intimidated the toddler uses biting freely as a defense against persons who interfere with his free activities. The emotion of hatred comes to life in connection with this primitive self-defense; the child impulsively fights for his newly found sense of freedom. It is highly important not to arouse and overstimulate these defensive activities. Later on, when his mind is more mature and he can understand necessary restrictions, the child will be ready to begin to restrain strong feelings of anger and hatred.

Another important area in which early emotions are aroused to a high pitch is toilet training. In this the toddler wants to take part and to direct himself. He resists coercion and strictness because, for the child of two, toilet training is a highly personal matter concerning his own body. Both positive and negative emotions may be aroused. Consideration and tact on the part of the trainer have a far-reaching effect. Most parents know that it is wise to put off the beginning of training to cleanliness until the child is well on in his second year and cooperates willingly because of his trust in his mother or nurse. Insistence on a fixed schedule for elimination and the use of force or punishment in this training create the contrary effect of arousing a defiance, a stubbornness, and a tendency to anger that is to most parents surprising. They do not recognize that a small child has a deep feeling about owning and directing his own body and its functions.

The toddler hates pain and is not yet able to understand any of its causes. When he is sick, he may scream and begin to struggle against a parent or a doctor who is examining him to find out what is the matter. He hates the doctor who, in examining the throat, ruthlessly forces his way in, rather than first winning the child's confidence and showing him what is to be done. Repeated explanations and demonstrations are necessary to reduce the fear of being hurt.

Painful punishment such as spankings unquestionably arouse hatred in a two-year-old. They foster his fantasies of dangerous giants, whom he cannot out-wit. He is too young to understand the meaning of a bodily attack and feels himself not only helpless but violated by the large and overbearing parent. Forcible restriction of the child's expressions of anger does not remove the anger but tends to build up repressed hatred. The small child has no ability to control his feelings until he has first used them and understood their effects.

The most important advice for parents is to avoid as far as possible situations which arouse anger and jeal-ousy. If they show amusement over the child's quick readiness to fight and over his sudden violent jealousies they produce a sense of confusion in the youngster and encourage the most primitive expressions of rage. Like the ancient Spartans and the not-so-remote Indians they are thereby fostering the spirit of fight and hatred and making it seem desirable. The natural impulse of the little child to bring into use all available defenses against another child who takes his toy or casually climbs into his mother's lap is indeed surprising and in-variably stirs amusement, but for the child it is serious and should not be taken lightly but rather objectively.

Bringing the intense feelings of a child into the grasp of his own understanding by means of free expression is a psychological accomplishment for which parents need definite preparation. An example will illustrate the point.

The parents of a little boy of two and a half asked for psychological help about a dramatic occurrence in the lives of all three. The father was a professor in a small university and the child's mother had been a successful kindergarten teacher. Dicky was an only child, reported as being exceptionally good until the time of this incident. The parents were giving a reception to the faculty of the university, the first social entertainment since the child's birth. It was planned for nine in the evening so that the child would be fed and put to bed in a quiet room upstairs at the usual hour of seven.

Elaborate preparations for the entertainment were in progress during the day without disturbing the usual routine of the child. He had asked questions about the cooking, the flowers in the house, and particularly the washing and setting out on the dining table of a valuable set of fine china. His mother explained to him in some detail that these were beautiful dishes which she kept for friends that she liked very much who were coming in to a party in the evening.

The child showed great interest, wanted to finger

the delicate china, and finally was tactfully diverted by his friend the cook who brought him a freshly baked cupcake. On a walk with his mother in the afternoon he again asked several times about the "beautiful dishes."

He was put to bed as usual by his father who dutifully told him a story before he went to sleep. As it happened the story was about a friend who was coming to the party, with whom the father had played when he himself was a little boy. The child was then left alone to go to sleep.

Just as the first guests were arriving a neighbor rang the doorbell and explained in some excitement that Dick was sitting on the window ledge in the dining room hurling dishes into her back-yard. He was quietly rescued by his father and put back to bed. The attentive and friendly cook brought up some ice cream in the one cup remaining from the two dozen thrown out the window. "That's my cup," exclaimed the child excitedly as he reached for it, but he was unable to eat his favorite ice cream and seemed to be greatly frightened. "Why did you throw away our nice dishes?" his father asked as gently as he could. There was a long silence, then the loud reply: "Don't like your beautiful friends." This youngster was emotion-

ally starved, hence he could not tolerate his parents'
expression of affection for others. On this basis his
panic of jealousy is understandable.

"What can be wrong with our youngster?" asked
the parents. "We try to understand him and we give
him so much." "Is my baby going to become a destructive and unruly child?" asked the mother (the
kindergarten teacher whose pride had been hurt and
who felt threatened by the thought that she might be
a failure with her own little son). The dignified and
very intelligent professor was even more distressed and
the immediate question that he asked was more shock-
ing: "Then is it possible that this destructive episode
means that my son is mentally defective?" Neither
parent could grasp the fact that the child had a deep
unformulated longing to find expressions of love for
himself which he could understand, to be warmly
loved, to be "special friends" with his own parents.

This rather tragic situation is not infrequent among
parents who are highly educated and make earnest attempts to do the *right thing* for their children but are
unable to communicate love to the child. In subsequent discussions of the troublesome incident it became clear that these parents had little understanding
of the child's emotional needs and even less of their
own emotional coldness. The lives of both had been

dominated by intellectual ambitions. They had read a great deal about "child psychology," and felt themselves well equipped and in a good situation to educate Dicky, but both were convinced that the frank showing of emotion was a weakness. Unknown to themselves they had a forbidding attitude which made this young child afraid to express the most natural and important feelings of his age. He had kept them to himself, releasing them only in the presence of his friend the cook. Hence an outburst of pent-up energy was necessary.

Emotion in human life is an energy of great value and serves as an important stimulus to the child's intelligence. As he begins to love those who understand him, his curiosity is aroused and he wants to know more about these people and all that they are and do. The first urges to learn gather much of their intensity from the emotions.

The child who loves well will learn well, provided the development of his early feeling life has been understood and guided from babyhood. Refusal to learn may begin as defiance toward parents who are hated because they have not recognized the child's need for love.

seven

THE ROOTS OF CHARACTER

A child who has reached the age of four or five and has had consistent and understanding parental guidance has naturally outgrown most of his infantile ways and is ready to accept the guidance of his parents in such basic principles as honesty, love of truth, personal modesty, and regard for the rights and feelings of family members and playmates. In other words, the roots of his character are well established; he has recognition and some acceptance of definite standards of behavior. He has become aware of a variety of satisfactions outside his own person: the pride of his parents in his achievements, in what he can do and in what he knows; the fun of good companionship with playmates; participating in family life; going places with daddy and having new things explained; and the feeling of importance which comes from being a loved and valued member of the family group and making a contribution to its comfort.

Character grows spontaneously from within through the process of psychological identification with parents on whom he is completely dependent. A dramatic illustration of this identification may be read in the story of the Wolf Child compiled by Dr. Gesell from notes given him by a missionary in Bengal, India. Here it is said to be not uncommon for a prowling female wolf with a litter of suckling pups to kidnap a human infant left to sleep outdoors while the mother works and to carry it off to her den. The story of Kamala tells of such a child, a girl, found in a wolf's den when she was at the estimated age of eight. She had adopted the ways of her wolf parents, walked on all fours, ran nimbly in the position of a quadruped, hunted with the pack at night and ate raw meat. Her language was the wolf howl that brought her meager security. Discovered by hunters and taken to an orphanage (run by a missionary and his wife) this human child crouched in a corner, snarled and bared her teeth in true wolflike fashion when approached. It took three years and the aid of massage by her foster mother before she could stand erect and walk. She used words clearly after four years, and was able to relinquish her accustomed wolf howl at three A.M. About the same time she began to show affection for the other children and enjoyed being allowed to take care of the younger ones. She also showed love for the foster parents at this time and began to live like a human being.

An important requisite for a child's early character growth is confidence in the goodness of his own body and its functions. He feels best physically and emotionally when his personality is kept in balance, when he is able with help to restrain anger and hatred, when he does not lose himself in daydreams—and when he does not solace himself on meeting unpleasant realities or disappointments by erotic play with his own body. He can then turn naturally to well-established ego interests as substitute satisfactions.

A positive attitude in parents is all-important in presenting social and moral ideals. Their conviction of the child's basic goodness must constantly be emphasized. They must present to him a dramatic and convincing picture of his progressive growth into a well-loved, interesting, and intelligent person, who can know a great deal, go to interesting places, and have nice things—above all, good friends. When too much emphasis is placed on warnings about making himself sick or the unpleasant things that may happen if he is "bad," character growth becomes difficult. These are not the years to present the negative aspects of life such as retribution (that is, punishment), illness, or want.

For example, Johnny, aged five, is thrilled at the prospects of what his birthday will bring him. His father, concerned that he will become too greedy and grasping, decides to point a moral; he offers to tell him a bedtime story. Johnny replies, "Yes, but please don't tell about bad boys, or some that got sick, or about poor children who don't get any things for their birthdays." In a way the child is right. Inevitably he will come in contact with the negative aspects of life in the next few years and they can then be talked through with him and some of their meaning explained. A child's anticipation of the pleasant things that life can bring is often spoiled by insistent moralizing.

Parents who are overly concerned about whether or not a young child tells the exact truth need to remind themselves that mental life, even at the age of four or five, may be still dominated by fantasy. The average youngster thinks much of the time in terms of the way he would like things to be rather than with serious intent to know how they actually are. When a young child persistently tells untruths it is usually an indication that he has suffered too much stress from parental disapproval and has taken refuge in day dreaming because of his fear of loss of love.

A little girl of two and a half, during the process of getting bladder control, occasionally "made puddles" on the floor. On hearing that a neighbor's daughter of the same age never wet herself in the daytime, her father decided to spank her when this occurred and to "make an end once and for all to this infantile lack of cooperation." Two spankings were administered, not severe, but none the less humiliating to the child. To his surprise the wetting increased. Coming home late one afternoon he found an unmistakable spot on the living-room rug. With some irritation he brought the protesting little one in and pointed to the spot. "Did you do that?" "No, daddy, doggie make puddle." "Why, you little liar!" the exasperated father shouted, and spanked again with considerable vigor. A long series of evasions followed until at the age of five the parents asked for psychological help. Their complaint was that "*since the age of two* the child has been deceitful and evasive," and "has not seemed to grasp the meaning of telling the truth."

Psychological therapy was begun, and in the weeks that followed the fantasies dynamically concerned in the problem of bladder control gradually came to light.

In the little girl's second year her mother had undergone a long and serious illness and a good deal of the care of the child fell to the father. He was inordinately proud of her intelligence but was unaware of the need for privacy in children of her age or of the harm that may result from too great an intimacy with adults. The father had allowed her to come into the bathroom while he showered and shaved and had frequently urinated in her presence. This intimacy aroused in her an exaggerated erotic interest in his body; she imagined herself urinating the way he did and was disturbed that her body was not exactly like his. Punishments for this "organic" expression of her love for him meant painful rejection and became the chief cause of her subsequent evasiveness and of the disturbance of progressive development of bladder control. When parents mistrust a child because of his frequent bragging or improvising of stories, the tendency increases rapidly because, to the child, mistrust means loss of parental affection.

"Telling stories on" a brother or sister of whom he

is jealous—believing that he gets more privileges and hence more love—is a frequent form of defense taken up by a small child. This early mud-slinging is an unfortunate defense mechanism which tends to weaken integrity of character and to put the child in a poor light with siblings and playmates. It is the task of parents to discover wherein they are responsible for the emotional lack that has inclined the child to use these tactics.

The cure lies in reassuring the jealous child that there is plenty of love for all, and in planning ways in which fair competition—through personal achievement and not through rivalry for love—may go on. In any case making an issue of truth-telling before school age is a defeatist gesture. In order that a youngster may develop a sense of truth and justice it is necessary that parents answer his questions truthfully and that they express trust in his *goodness*. A small child who has been confronted with an excess of unpleasant reality—as parental disagreements, fault-finding and censure, arguments about principles of child-training —will counter painful scenes by evasion. He may weave them into fantasies of dangerous giants and wicked witches.

One of the fundamental and highly desirable character traits to foster in a child is recognition of the rights of others and consideration for their feelings. An outgoing and friendly social attitude is an asset to the small child and a necessity for successful community living later on. Human beings who achieve and maintain completeness of personality development are closely dependent on each other. Because of the long period of infancy during which the child is almost wholly dependent on his parents, he has an innate readiness to form attachments. If the relationship with parents and siblings has been warm and reassuring, he will anticipate warmth and reassurance from other human beings.

Actually, the child's attitude toward others is fundamentally a reflection of his parents' attitude toward him. Whether positive or negative, this basic attitude grows during the early years, is deeply etched in the mind, and begins to show itself some time later. Readiness to share with brothers and sisters his sweets and toys and, later, parental affection, and finally to extend this generosity to playmates, depends in no small way on the manner in which the parents have guided the early stages of the child's maturing.

Respect for parents and for adults in general cannot be inculcated by means of a command or authority. It comes about through having been understood, helped, and respected all along the way to becoming a social person. Self-respect is a good basis on which to build respect for others. Ideally the self-love of the child extends, little by little, into love of family and the gradually increasing capacity to give and receive affection. The child soon finds that continued self-interest arouses in his playmates dislike and a determination to "get even." The social sense grows best in good family life, where it is possible to substitute companionship with brothers and sisters for the *complete possessiveness* of parents. In this fashion, the roots of social living are planted and grow into widening group relationships.

The child who insists on having his own way usually has a weak spot within himself that makes him fearful. "Meanness" invariably indicates this sort of weakness against which he is fighting but which he cannot overcome. This "meanness" is very different from the love of cruelty exhibited by a two-year-old who has not had help in deflecting his early aggressiveness and his wishes for power.

The quality of modesty and need for restraint of sex impulses increases as the school age is approached. When the attitude of the parents toward sex development has been frank from the beginning, when excessive fondling has not been indulged in (particularly kissing on the mouth), when there has been due regard for personal privacy and sleeping with someone else has been avoided, the youngster will assume reasonable control of himself with a minimum of effort. Under these conditions, modesty will be based on a degree of self-understanding, on confidence in parental guidance, a desire to cooperate, and on the ability to get satisfaction from companionship with playmates and from learning. Otherwise, this modesty will be the undesirable product of parental prudishness or crippling inhibitions.

The child, who, from lack of guidance, is unable or unwilling to practice such restraint, usually pursues his natural sex interests in secret. The exaggerated feeling of guilt thus resulting is an inhibiting force in personality growth. The feeling of strength and confidence gained by the toddler when he is free to move his body about and is able to direct his bowel and bladder functions is a basic factor in his ability to control, in later years, his sex impulses. When parents have interfered with these natural body functions or have attempted to train the child too early or too vigorously, the developing control system is weakened. Another factor which we have already stressed in this connection is that if diarrhea or constipation have been frequent or long-continued without relief, the sexual sensitiveness of the child is increased and he finds it difficult to gain control of his bodily interests.

The concept of "stealing," when applied to a child of three or four, is entirely inappropriate. If at this time he persistently takes things which belong to other children, it usually means that he has experienced too many deprivations and probably he is not getting enough affection to feel sure of himself and secure in his family relationship. Continuous discipline and punishment tend to increase the painful feeling that nobody loves him. It is better not to condemn the child for "stealing," but to take each incident as it occurs and talk it through carefully. The child will often give a clue as to where his unhappiness lies and why he finds it necessary to take things from other children. Respect for the possessions of others comes easier to a child who has been taught how to take care of what belongs to him, but it depends even more on his feeling that he belongs to and has the approval of just and loving parents.

The child of three, on a visit to the home of a friend or taken by his mother to a store, may artlessly help himself to something that appeals to him. This is natural behavior for his age and does not in any way indicate something amiss within the child. However, it may lead to a frightening experience for him if the adults concerned do not accept this behavior as completely normal. The annoyed friend or a menacing salesman may confuse the child and may make the parent extremely uncomfortable or downright alarmed. It is vitally important to avoid incidents of this kind. Immediately following such an occurrence a quiet and simple explanation to the child of the difference between "mine" and "yours" is good procedure. The wise parent or friend will guard against repetition by giving the child a treat rather than by further depriving him.

Parents occasionally ask "What are some of the things that go wrong in the early stages of character growth?" Sometimes it is hard for parents to accept the fact that the young child is good by nature but must be protected from experiences that thwart or work against his natural goodness. There is constant evidence of an inner urge to grow out of infantile ways after they have been fully exercised and their function has been fulfilled. There is also constant evidence of the child's readiness to be promoted to the next stage of maturing.

However, ambitious parents find it hard to fall in with the idea that there is no skipping of grades in the early maturing process. The child will adapt himself easily and naturally under good leadership, but he cannot be hurried. Growth and maturing make large demands on all his energies and an inner balance must be maintained if body and mind are to grow smoothly and evenly.

Hence, when a three-year-old frequently becomes irritable and loses control he should not be considered a *bad* child. His outbursts may mean that his nervous system is exhausted by the demands upon it from overexcitement. Blood sugar may be low, or the calcium necessary for rapid bone-building may not be sufficient. Moreover, the young body cannot always distribute supplies quickly and efficiently. The situation is somewhat like that of an adult who is convalescing from a long illness and whose tissues are being repaired. He easily becomes fatigued and feels tense. The same is true of a pregnant woman who often experiences a similar tension because of the high demands made upon her body by the growing embryo. The adult does, however, have the advantage of knowing how and when he will get relief, while, on the other hand, the child has no understanding of the reasons for his discomfort.

Another area in which adults experience disappointment and frequently condemn a child is in his strong dependency on the presence of his parents. Reaction to loneliness which a youngster is unable to verbalize is frequently mistaken for "badness." At the age of two or three a child may be overwhelmed by longing for his parents who have gone on a trip. He has been told emphatically, "You must be good while we are away"; but mother's lap and father's hand are the security by which he grows. His mind cannot yet grasp the fact that the separation will be short, or that the distance is not great, and that they can return quickly if needed, much less the fact that they are tired and need a rest. Emotional need, like persistent hunger, is little tolerated in early life and if not gratified results after a time in reversion to the simpler instinctual forms of satisfaction—thumb-sucking or masturbation—or to some form of destructiveness, such as nail-biting and hair-twisting. This does not indicate bad character.

The successful cure for these trying disturbances of progress is often made by tactfully and consistently reestablishing a warm and companionable relationship by means of which the child's fears of separation or of not being loved are allayed. Character training can easily deteriorate into policing, persistent mistrust, and spying, or a gloomy system of warnings and threats. These methods invariably lead to defeat. Character is not learned by indoctrination and punishment, and it must not be a veneer which covers something ugly or untrue underneath.

eight

CHILD AND PARENT (IN RETROSPECT)

Some of the gains to a child who has been given genuine companionship with parents is his happy and full development. Before he reaches school age he has already acquired considerable understanding of himself and some of the security which comes because he is not in danger of being overwhelmed by his own instinctual desires within or by requirements from his parents which are beyond his capacity. He has the rudiments of sex education and feels free to express his urgent curiosity to family members because no one says to him, "You shouldn't even think such things." He is well along in the process of learning that fights are emergency measures against cruelty, stupidity, or infringements of his personal freedom. A happy disposition toward life causes him to anticipate the best from friends and relatives, so he often gets it. On this basis he is able to tolerate temporary pain or disappointment without recourse to fantasy or to artificial defenses. His thinking is free, urgent, and enjoyable. This makes him ready to learn from teachers, who become substitute parents in the best sense. He has an eagerness to know many schoolmates and will love a few.

Such a healthy and dynamic personality does not give way under the inevitable pressures and strains which develop later in life. It is resilient and will usually find a comeback.

A touching compliment to her parents was overheard from a five-year-old girl giving solace to a younger companion who was painfully grappling with her doubts in Santa Claus. "Silly, can't you understand who Santa Claus really is? He's your own father and mother who like to dress up, the way we do sometimes, and surprise us with nice things. Isn't that okay? They used to do it for us babies who couldn't even understand how much their fathers and mothers really loved them. Now they do it just for fun."

This youngster could accept reality, which implied a threat of loss to her younger companion, because consistent experience with her parents had assured her that love is a good solution and leads to understanding.

Parents, in turn, who have been able to equip themselves with the additional knowledge and skill necessary to guide young human nature will have many rewards. Aside from the obvious joy in an emotionally well-adjusted child, they will have the satisfaction of knowing that a personality whose instinctual and emotional roots are strong and well knit will continue to grow and flourish. The child's intelligence thus has some of the push of instinct behind it. These innate energies which contribute drive to the mental life have not been isolated as dangerous but are flowing in reasonable harmony with the best ideals of self. The child's first reasoning is well mixed with love.

In addition, parents will find themselves better educated, more tolerant, free from self-love, and increasingly able to free the child from dependency. Such parents will not expect from the child in later life a talion return for what they have generously given.

books

FOR FURTHER READING

Childhood and Society, by Erik H. Erikson.
W. W. NORTON & COMPANY, INC., 1950.
Anthropological studies of parent-child attitudes accompany detailed genetic presentations of personality development with case material.

The Lost and the Found, by Robert Collis.
WOMAN'S PRESS, WHITESIDE, INC., 1953.

A moving story of two war orphans lost in the horrors of Nazi persecution who came under the care of an Irish army doctor and were finally adopted by him. Deep disturbances of personality are described as well as the transformation which took place because of a good start in early life.

The Early Years of Life, by Alice Balint.
BASIC BOOKS, INC., 1954.

A psychoanalytic study of some of the problems in early childhood. It is in technical language and would be most useful to parents who have undergone psychoanalysis.

War and Children, by Anna Freud and D. Burlingham.
INTERNATIONAL UNIVERSITY PRESS, 1944.

A highly valuable study of aggression in young children and of the ways it is affected by their experiences in a world war.

The Emotional Problems of Living, by O. Spurgeon English, M.D., and Gerald H. J. Pearson, M.D.
W. W. NORTON & COMPANY, INC., 1945.

This detailed discussion of emotional development is written from the psychoanalytic point of view. It covers the entire life of the individual and includes problems of emotional illness and something about their treatment.

The Normal Sex Interests of Children, by Frances Bruce Strain.
APPLETON-CENTURY-CROFTS, INC., 1948.
An interesting little book written by a teacher who has had experience with children of all ages.

Wolf Child and Human Child, by Arnold Gesell, M.D.
HARPER & BROTHERS, 1941.
The extremely interesting though somewhat disturbing story of a human child kidnapped by a wolf. It describes the wolf ways of the child and the process of reeducating her to human feeling and human ways of living.

Three Contributions to the Theory of Sex, by Sigmund Freud.
NERVOUS AND MENTAL DISEASE PUBLISHING CO., 1930.
Original source material on childhood sexuality. It should be read carefully by every parent who has had some scientific training.

The Embryology of Behavior, by Arnold Gesell, M.D.
HARPER & BROTHERS, 1945.

Chapters 7 and 8 describe with great scientific accuracy the physiological development of breathing and the establishing of muscle tone, fundamental somatic factors in personality development.